SURVIVAL!

Geoff R. Moon,

Bill Johnston
Jean Johnston

Published by

White Rose Books

79-81 Market Place, Thirsk,
North Yorkshire YO7 1ET

ISBN: 0 9544871 0 9

We gratefully acknowledge SFB Photography
for the photographs used on the front and back cover.

Printed and Bound in Great Britain by
MAXIPRINT
Kettlestring Lane, Clifton Moor, York YO30 4XF

SURVIVAL!

by Geoff. R. Moore

Published by

White Rose Books

'A memory is a short thing.'
Wing Commander Guy Gibson, V.C., D.S.O., D.F.C.

This story is dedicated to those who did not return.

Contents

Chapter One

On the 21st January, 1944 the log of Pilot Officer William Johnston read 'missing'. Records at Linton-on-Ouse R.A.F. Station in Yorkshire stated 'killed in action'. A telegram received by his wife Joan read: 'Information received through the International Red Cross Committee that Pilot Officer William Johnston is a prisoner-of-war in German hands.' Only one told the truth.

Bill Johnston's story begins in the aftermath of the First World War. The 'war to end wars' had reached its bloody conclusion on the 11th of November,1918 with the signing of the Armistice. Bill's father had served as an artilleryman in France. Fortunately, he was neither gassed nor injured but the mental experiences he had undergone were to live with him for the rest of his life. He returned from the conflict to marry his sweetheart, Hannah. Accommodation for those returning from the war was in short supply, Belfast was no exception. However, a solution was to hand, for above a shoe repair shop in the Shankill Road lived Hannah's mother, Sarah. Four rooms occupied the space above the shop and it was decided that the newly-weds should share two. The rooms were not large. In one of the rooms a cold tap above a stone sink provided water for cooking and washing. What food there was, was cooked on a coal range which also provided heat. Stone steps led from one of the rooms to a back yard. Here, in a corner, was the toilet. Furnishings in the two rooms were sparse, a table, chairs and a cupboard, all donated, were to be found in one of the rooms, while a bed occupied the other. A permanent smell of gas pervaded the air. This smell emanated from the gas lights, for gas mantles were easily broken and expensive. Not only was there a problem with the lights but the taps controlling the supply did not always function and this added to the seepage of gas.

Eleven days before Christmas in 1919 Bill Johnston was born. This was Hannah's first-born and the birth of a boy was greeted with jubilation.

Bill's dad had a steady if unrewarding job with the Corporation. He did, however, have a great singing voice which was much in demand during festivities and home entertainment. Other children followed and soon the two rooms above the shop became more and more cramped. Eventually rooms nearby were found and the Johnston family, apart from Bill, moved to new accommodation. Bill was to continue to live above the shop with Sarah, his grandmother. Hannah called daily to ensure her first-born did not forget either his parents or his brothers and sisters. Hannah was not the only visitor for family ties were strong and never a day passed without some relative calling in.

Young Bill Johnston soon learned to crawl and talk. He was fascinated by the glow of the coal fire and the open-flamed gas lights with their blue and white flames which hissed, spluttered and flickered long into the night. On occasions the rooms above the shop would be crowded with relatives and neighbours all intent on having a good time. Now and then a jug of beer would be sent for and this seemed to add to the merriment of the sing-a-longs and the story telling. For a while the adults would put away their worries about family, money and work. On other occasions Bill would use the cracked doors and holes in the floor boards as a listening post or spyhole to discover what was being said and who was saying what. Much of what he overheard meant little to him.

Like other youngsters in the Shankill Road, Bill was educated by his religion. Such religion split the population into polarised groups – Protestants and Catholics. Catholics were born Nationalists, while Protestants were born Unionists. Bill claims that there was blind obedience to whatever religion you were born into. Church life was important to the people of the Shankill. Denominations of all types flourished and contributed to the bustling life of the Road. Though his education began at home, a more formal education began with his association with the church and with school.

The thought of school filled Bill with foreboding. His playmates had already filled Bill's mind with tales of a regime where discipline was harsh. He was not to be disappointed. The scampering feet in the playground were brought to a sudden and jarring halt by the sound of a whistle blown by the teacher. Not a sound was heard as the eyes of the master swept the statue-like children. On a second blast, lines were formed and the young Johnston was hastily shoved into a line of infants. Then Bill received his first, but not his last, orders to march with head up and chest out. He was escorted by those in front and behind into a brick-built building with high windows, whose only view was to leaden skies and slates of grey. Allocated a place in a dual desk with fixed seats, Bill gazed at the charts on the wall, the blackboard and easel and the master's desk on which reposed that instrument of discipline 'the cane'.

As if it was second nature, Bill sat up straight with folded arms and awaited events.

A routine was established of writing with pencils on slates framed with wood, chanting tables, reading aloud and reciting poetry. Throughout his school life such a routine seldom changed. The emphasis was on the three R's – reading, writing and arithmetic and woe betide those who did not try and did not sit up straight with arms folded. For Bill, school seemed a contradiction – harsh discipline yet a wealth of knowledge waiting to be imparted and absorbed.

School was where you were taught Protestant History, Protestant Geography, English, Arithmetic and Art. An alert Bill realised that he was receiving a lop-sided education for no-one bothered, as a Prodi, with Catholic Dublin. Of school uniform there was none. Boots or bare feet sufficed as footwear, socks if one had them. Short trousers were the order of the day, while jerseys supplied a covering for the upper body. Bill remembers a longing to go to school as a bare-footed youngster, a thought which would have horrified both his mother and grandmother. The streets along which Bill travelled to his first educational establishment were noisy, dirty and smelly. Smoke belched from factory chimneys and it was this smoke, coupled with that from the myriad domestic dwellings, that meant the sun rarely shone on the Shankill Road. Bill could not, at this stage of his life, understand the slateless skeletons of roofs and the reason for the dismal streets. He much preferred the maps which adorned the walls of his classroom and which, he believed, promised a more colourful life. Bill's mother produced seven more children – two girls and five boys. As each arrived, Bill became further bewildered as to his own situation. However, a new sport appeared to enliven his life, for while at school Bill was introduced to the art of boxing. It proved a useful skill to possess for, like all young boys, he was frequently involved in fights.

The Government of Ireland Act (1920) had gone some way towards placating the deep divisions between the various religious and political beliefs of the people of Ireland – often referred to as the 'troubles'. This resulted in the establishment of Southern Ireland with its own Parliament and independence. Northern Ireland would also retain its parliament but still owe an allegiance to the British Government. Not a really satisfactory solution, for the 'troubles' would continue to rumble on. In Belfast, especially in areas like the Shankill Road, a slow slum clearance was under way as unhealthy property was demolished and new housing built. As a result there was plenty of waste ground. The kids at the top of Shankill Road made full use of such ground. Marking out goals for football or knocking in bits of wood as stumps for a game of cricket was commonplace. Many a game exceeded the numbers officially allowed and many a ball was simply a collection of material shaped and bound with string. Bill recalls his delight at being asked to join 'a gang'. It all sounded very mysterious but he quickly learned that on the Shankill there was safety in numbers.

At the age of seven Bill was accepted as a member of the Life Boys. This was the Junior section of the Boys Brigade and Bill would, at the age of eleven, transfer to this senior arena. The Boys Brigade had been founded by William A. Smith. Its motto was 'Sure and Stedfast'. The activities it encouraged met with a ready response from many of the lads in the Shankill Road. William A. Smith's keynote belief was that the advancement of Christ's kingdom among boys could be encouraged by drill, physical exercises, obedience, punctuality, cleanliness and talks. It was hoped that as a result of such disciplines the boys would learn that they had duties and responsibilities, not only to themselves, but to others. The movement was based on an army structure of squads, platoons, companies, and battalions with army ranks allocated to those who had the necessary knowledge and experience. The simple uniform of a brown leather waist belt with the crest of an anchor on the buckle, a white haversack and a dark blue hat with two narrow braidings and worn at a tilt was something Bill never possessed. This did not lessen his enthusiasm for the movement. Meetings for this more senior branch were held weekly in the church hall. Competitions and drill were the order of the day. Bill and his pals were put into groups and drilled in the art of marching.

In 1933 the Boys Brigade celebrated its Golden Jubilee with a camp at Glasgow between the 8th and 11th of September. Two boys from every company in the Brigade were invited to represent their comrades at this event. Unfortunately, Bill was not one of those selected. He did, however, attend his own Brigade's camp at Millisle on the Irish coast. This was an annual semi-military adventure where bell tents were pitched in line and the boys slept with feet pointing towards the central pole. A dining tent was erected and a central cooking area was established. Bill's day would begin with reveille at 6.30a.m. followed by morning prayers. The day would continue with bathing, breakfast, inspection and a parade. Dinner would be about one o'clock and in the afternoon would be games or rambles. Such games encouraged discipline coupled with competition and enjoyment. Tea would be taken 6.30p.m. and following this hymns and songs would be sung round a camp fire. Lights out would be at ten o'clock. Discipline, Bill recalls, was fairly tight but the clean air of Millisle and the food did wonders for those who, like Bill, benefited from such an experience.

By the age of nine Bill knew that religion dominated the Shankill Road. It seemed to be a road pulsating with hatred. Hatred seeped from the

Bill Johnston attending a Boys Brigade camp in 1933. Bill is wearing a badge in his coat lapel.

bricks from which the very dwellings were made. Not unfamiliar with sectarian riots and feuds, he watched as the gable-ends of houses were painted with pictures and slogans. Such efforts were in preparation for the march of the Orangemen which took place on the 12th of July. These men were members of the Loyal Orange Order and proclaimed loyalty to the British Crown as long as the monarchy remained Protestant. The 12th of July was important to this Order, for on that date in 1690, William of Orange was victorious over the Catholic English King James the Second, in the Battle of the Boyne. With their bowler hats, sashes, pipe bands, silver bands, drums and waving banners, they presented a sense of majesty to young Bill. Perhaps, for the young, the night before the parade was the night to capture their imagination. For weeks, children of the Road had been collecting anything that would burn. Such material was piled on any vacant waste ground or even on the road itself as each street and road vied with the other for the largest bonfire. Such was the rivalry that often the youngsters slept as sentinels alongside their precious collections. Great was the cheer when evening came and a match was put to the pile. The ascending flames and smoke, along with the dancing sparks, made for excitement beyond compare. The great bonus as the flames died was the baking of potatoes in the embers. Great daring was needed as the potatoes, which had been scrounged from parents and relatives, were thrust into the dying fire. Anxious, smoke-filled eyes would watch as the skin of the potatoes blackened until, with a stick, they were eventually raked from the embers. So hot were they that many a hand was burned as the roasted potatoes were split open in order to consume the wonderful contents. Not all were successful for many potatoes were thrust into the fire with such high hopes only to be consumed by a sudden burst of flame from what should have been a dying fire. The shrieks of the children challenged the shouts of the adults. It was a great night.

Throughout the provinces of Northern Ireland August was associated with school holidays. The Johnstons were a close-knit family and it was rightly believed that a spell at the coast would do young Bill no harm – no harm at all. His Aunt Lizzie, from a more prosperous side of the family, used to rent a house at Donaghadee. With her two daughters, her son Joe and Bill they would journey by train to this seaside resort.

Donaghadee, on the north east coast of Northern Ireland with its beach, its pier, its woodlands and its entertainment was, to a small boy, a great place to be. The routine seldom varied. The first activity of the morning was a swim in the sea. This was not a question of dipping your toe in to see if it was cold but to swim for five or ten minutes in the sea. Accompanying such a swim would be the words: 'It's good for you' Afterwards, shivering blue bodies danced up and down trying to get warm. Games would then be organised and these would be interspersed with walks, either in the nearby woodland or along the beach. Mealtimes were strictly adhered to and the rule at tea was: 'If you have jam you can't have butter and if you have butter you can't have jam.'

From Donaghadee you could see the West Coast of Scotland. Bill recalls an American swimmer, Miss Gilchrist, emerging from the sea having just swum from Port Patrick. No mean feat and many claimed much more difficult than swimming the English Channel.

Other outings claimed some of Bill Johnston's time. As a regular attender at Sunday School he was entitled to go on the summer outings to either Portrush or Newcastle. Excitement for such outings would build in the minds of those lucky enough to participate. The preparation of a small boy for such excursions was intense. Hands, face and legs would be washed, threats made against any form of misbehaviour, and finally a quick hug was given. On arrival at their destination Bill and his friends were under the watchful eyes of the Sunday School teachers. Each outing was organised with almost military precision. Games would be played, sandwiches eaten and lemonade drunk. Just to get away from the smoke-filled air of the Shankill Road was a bonus in itself. One of his delights on such days was to scrounge a cigarette, climb a tree and blow smoke in the direction of those in holy orders. He was not alone.

Talk on such outings would frequently turn to the stage and screen star George Formby. George, with his ukulele and his buck teeth, was a firm favourite of the Irish youth. Bill, along with thousands of other children, believed that all English folk had buck teeth. Motor-cycle racing, similar to that held on the Isle of Man was organised twice a year on the outskirts of Belfast. Here, after a penny tram ride and a good walk, the noise of revving engines would assail the ears. Bill enjoyed such excursions for watching motor-cyclists speed round an improvised track would evoke excitement in the minds of the young.

Family ties were strong. Grandmother Sarah died when Bill was twelve. Hannah, his mother, died shortly afterwards and it was Bill's father, helped by an aunt, who brought the family up. As a result of his work at school, Bill had also gained entrance to the local Technical College. However, costs prohibited him from capitalising on his success.

As Bill grew up, part-time work beckoned. His foray into this was first by running errands for various members of the family. This progressed to helping out in a shop run by one of his aunts. One of the more eccentric shop owners that Bill remembers was an undertaker. A great one for advertising his services, he was renowned for his odd publicity. One such advertisement that Bill remembers read: 'Why live when I can bury you for £12.' To many of the limbless men who had returned from the trenches and who hawked their wares along the Shankill it was a thoroughly tempting offer. The only problem was lack of money.

The cinema offered a way of escape. Adventure and romance flourished on the screen as Joan Crawford, Greta Garbo, Clark Gable and Gene Autry wove their spells. A local cinema, known affectionately as The Ranch, soon captured Bill's imagination. Here, for two jam jars or one penny, you could watch cowboy films. This cinema in the Crumlin Road was noted for the manager's enthusiasm for the Wild West. He would frequently be seen, dressed as a cowboy, quelling the rowdy youngsters with imaginary pistol shots. The Hippodrome and Empire provided live entertainment, here Sophie Tucker and Harry Lauder would perform. A ticket for the 'gods' would cost sixpence but when you could afford such a sum it was money well spent.

Money was desperately short. There was none to spend on cigarettes and it was a sin to encourage a girl's feelings. For the cost of a penny you could travel into the centre of Belfast. The tram would clank and rattle along the gas-lit roads past the shops filled with goods Bill couldn't afford. A supporter of Linfield Football Club, Bill and his mates would frequently be lifted over the turnstile in order to watch a match. Once in the ground the young would be passed over the heads of the adults down to the front. Here they would get a good view. One of the most famous Irish players Bill saw was Joe Bambrick. He would join in the chanting of, 'Head, heel or toe, slip it to Joe.' It was at Linfield's ground that he saw the international stars of England, Scotland and Wales. After the match if he had enough money it would be spent on a plate of chips from the café at Woolworths. Yet another attraction in the city of Belfast was boxing. Periodically a Mrs. Copley, accompanied by a number of professional boxers, would set up her circus tent on ground used by the fair people. Before advertising her programme she would walk the area offering a pound or two to those who would join a mismatch bout. Such mismatches would often involve tall men boxing short men or fat men (difficult to find) versus thin men,(easy to find). Once she had enough takers she would announce the evening's entertainment. One of the mismatch favourites was 'Birdseed' Crichton, so named because he kept a pet shop and was always whistling. 'Birdseed' always fancied his chances in the ring. One of his tricks was to fill his mouth with water during one of the three rounds. When his opponent was least expecting it 'Birdseed' would squirt a mouthful of water in his face. Such action used to bring mayhem to the boxing booth. Still, it was always good entertainment.

In contrast to such leisure, Bill also attended the Shankill Road Mission which he knew as the 'Albert Hall'. This mission had been the brainchild of the Reverend Henry Montgomery, who was a

Presbyterian minister. The Rev. Henry, when he first visited the Shankill Road, had been shocked, not only by the drunkenness of many of the people but by their appalling living conditions. Concerned for their salvation and their health the Rev. Henry sought patrons to overcome such challenges. As a result the 'Albert Hall' was built. A huge building, it provided not only a very large meeting place but facilities for a reading library, a boys' club room, girls' guild room, medical area, ladies room, a dispensary together with places for twenty students in the Residential Training Club. The Shankill Road Mission Yearbook describes how over two thousand Christmas parcels, as well as clothing, blankets and coal, were distributed to the needy. All activities attracted a huge following and as Bill recalls from his visits to the mission, hope was given for the future.

As Bill grew up he frequently listened to gossip about those who had emigrated to America. Tales of a new life, a new climate and new opportunities for those who had crossed the ocean would last well into the night. Once in a while Bill and his mates would watch the boats taking people out of Belfast Lough to the waiting ships some ten miles down river. Such boats, known as lighters, were filled with potential emigrants bound for America or Canada. Songs such as 'Will ye no come back again' would be sung by those who had come to wave good-bye. Bill envied those who were crossing the ocean. Young Bill was told that once the migrants had landed in that far off land the Protestants would drift towards Ontario while the Catholics headed towards Boston and New England. Not all settled to a new way of life in a distant country. A number returned to the city they had left, sadder and wiser for the thousands of miles travelled.

To feed his enquiring mind Bill joined the library, a whole new world awaited him. Books on travel and books filled with adventure gripped his imagination. The wireless did not intrude on his life for his family did not possess one. His friend's family across the road did. This new form of communication and entertainment astounded those who gathered round the set. It was the wireless that provided news and entertainment as well as information. Silence reigned as the news was read, then absorbed and discussed. The name of Hitler was frequently read out but this did not worry young Bill and his mates. However, it was forbidden to listen to the wireless on a Sunday. Sunday was set aside for religion. This, coupled with poverty and an expected blind obedience to order, troubled young Bill. A thinking lad, he was conscious of the sectarian divide and the subsequent hatred stirred up by acts of violence. Such acts included intimidation, burning of property, sacking from employment and beatings. During Bill's early childhood Southern Ireland had been granted Home Rule. The six provinces of Northern Ireland stuck to their belief that they should continue to be part of the United Kingdom. Not all agreed, and segregation into Catholic and Protestant areas continued to dominate Belfast. Bill was aware of such feelings but any thoughts had to be shared with the exploits of 'Popeye' and the songs of George Formby.

Unemployment continued to be a problem in Belfast and it was decided that Bill should stay on an extra year at school. Poverty was a fact of life and the horses and carts which had dominated Shankill Road for years were slowly being replaced by motorised vehicles. These were not half as much fun, for a traditional sport of the young had been hanging on to the back of the carts to see how far they could travel before being spotted by the driver.

Replying to an advertisement in the paper, Bill was taken on as an apprentice by a local builder, McCosh. He was promised by the firm that he would be taught how to be a joiner but first he had to acquire the necessary tools of the trade. Such tools were expensive and almost beyond the reach of the Johnston family. One member of the family suggested that he approach an uncle who sold such tools. Hoping for a discount, he presented his list to his relative, only to be sold some inferior equipment with no discount. This was another lesson for the young school leaver that you get no favours in this world, not even from relatives.

This was a new way of life as Bill found himself working on a variety of sites. A keen observer of people, Bill realised he was not being treated fairly, for he was learning very little about being a joiner but a great deal about labouring. Always one to stand his ground he decided a move was necessary. This was to another building firm, Armeeds, where he found training in the art of building much better. To improve his knowledge and skill he studied carpentry and building in the evening at the Technical College.

Bill and his friends, whether at work or at leisure, had one burning ambition – to visit Blackpool. Conversation after conversation was dominated by this seaside wonderland with its attractions of the famous Tower, its six miles of sandy beaches, exhilarating amusements, fortune tellers, dance halls and girls. Dreams of dancing in the Tower ballroom with a girl in his arms, (although he could not dance) occupied Bill's thoughts for many hours. The only problem about getting to Blackpool it seemed was lack of money. However, there was a possible solution. The Territorial Army was advertising for recruits, coupled with the promise that after a period of time a cash bounty would be paid. Could this, Bill wondered, be the opportunity to get to that famous seaside resort of Blackpool?

Enquiries at the Territorial Barracks by Bill and his younger brother confirmed that indeed the Territorial Army was recruiting and that a bounty would be paid. Those in charge explained about the obligations of those who joined. Members of the Territorial Army were expected to attend weekly drills, learn about military weapons and present themselves at the annual camp. It was also explained that in the event of a national emergency, such as a declaration of war, those who enlisted would immediately be on full active service. The two young lads gave little thought to this aspect of life in the Territorials for somehow or other they were going to get to Blackpool and sample its delights. Bill's younger brother added a few years to his age and signatures were applied to the recruitment form. The Territorial Army gained two new recruits.

The attractions of the 3rd (Ulster) Anti-Aircraft Brigade (Supplementary Reserve) was that it promised not only adventure but also an opportunity to get away rather from a dull life. Issued with old-type army uniforms and puttees, Bill and his brother reported to the Balmoral Centre for training. The drilling and marching which accompanied each visit reinforced the discipline they had endured as members of the Boys Brigade.

During attendances at the Territorial Army Centre Bill listened to tales of the Great War as told by men who had returned from the trenches. The news of Germany's continued warlike threats uttered by Adolf Hitler made the old sweats mock Chamberlain's efforts to come to terms with Hitler. Bill began to enjoy the friendship of his fellow volunteers, although he had yet to claim his bounty and visit Blackpool. The annual camp loomed and Bill packed his kit bag. It was while at camp that the situation in Europe deteriorated still further and in June 1939 a state of emergency was declared. Bill was now on full-time active service, Blackpool he could only still dream about.

Chapter Two

Standing some five feet three inches tall Bill Johnston, with his clean shaven face and twinkling blue eyes, was transported, along with fellow Territorials, to the coastline of Northern Ireland. Tents were pitched in military fashion at Portstewart and guard duty began.

The recent bombing campaign by the Irish Republican Army in London, Manchester, Birmingham and Coventry meant that the Territorial unit was ordered to be vigilant, not only to possible attack by Germans but also against an assault by the I.R.A. Issued with rifles, Bill and his companions patrolled the coastline in shifts, some twenty four hours a day. Guard duty did not replace the other rituals of army life. Marching and drilling continued as did the regular inspections of kit. Duties were assigned, for the potatoes had to be peeled and the pans scrubbed. Weapon training was limited, for weapons of any type were in short supply. Card games flourished within the confines of the camp. It was dull routine work but considered necessary by those in command. There were numerous false alarms as exaggerated rumours spread from the local populace to the troops. One of the most persistent rumours was that German parachutists had landed and were already making inroads into the towns and cities of Northern Ireland. Talk revolved round Hitler and his creed of Nazi-ism which seemed to have captured the imagination of the German people. Great were the discussions that took place as the threat of war seemed to ebb and flow like the tide. Those who were members of the territorials and who had served in the 1914-1918 war regaled their comrades with tales of life in the trenches. There were many who now believed that war with Germany was inevitable and that the piece of paper Prime Minister Chamberlain had waved so proudly, proclaiming that Hitler had no intention of fighting a war against Great Britain, was a lie. Those members of the 3rd (Ulster) Anti-Aircraft Brigade who, along with Bill, visited the cinema in their time off were entertained by newsreels showing Germany's conflict with Finland. A new type of warfare was being developed and the Territorials felt ill-equipped. Still, as Bill remarked, 'they were in the army now,' and there was a sense of adventure in the air.

Further orders took Bill to Larne. Here the routine was the same but accommodation. better. A school hall, much to the delight of the pupils, had been commandeered, and to the Territorials was much more comfortable than a tented camp. The Territorials underwent additional training in what weapons were available. Larne, with its industry, port and social attractions, proved a much livelier place for the young men from the Shankill.

The rantings of Adolf Hitler continued to make headline news during the summer of 1939. Germany's politicians and many other Germans believed that not only had they been unfairly treated at the end of the 1914/18 war by the Treaty of Versailles but that much of Poland's territory rightly belonged to the German nation. The British and French Governments gave a guarantee of support to the Polish Government should an attempt be made to interfere with its independence.

On the first of September of 1939 German forces invaded Poland. A new type of warfare was developing with the German air force playing a dominant role. Dornier 17's and Heinkel 111's pounded Polish towns and cities. Following these attacks Stuka dive-bombers added their bomb loads to those already delivered. Communication systems, be they road, rail, canal or radio were destroyed. As if this wasn't enough, tanks, armoured cars, parachutists and infantry made rapid progress into Polish territory.

By this time Bill had travelled across the Irish Sea to Stranraer and then by train to Aldershot. The town was awash with troops as the threat of war with Germany continued to dominate the news. For the first time Bill was billeted in barracks. This was a new and interesting experience for the nineteen-year-old. One such experience lives with him to this day. During the night a soldier had come in drunk and urinated into Bill's boots. Great was his outrage when he had to put them on. Training continued daily and the delights of Aldershot were denied the platoon as they learned to drill, tackle obstacle courses and undergo route marches. Perhaps the most farcical aspect of training was the throwing of hand grenades in the barrack room. Such grenades were in fact tennis balls as no grenades were available.

At 11.15a.m. on the 3rd of September the British Prime Minister, Neville Chamberlain, spoke to the nation on the wireless. In a voice full of despair he said, 'I am speaking to you from the Cabinet Room at No. 10 Downing Street. This morning, the British Ambassador in Berlin handed the German government a final note, stating that unless the British government heard from them by 11 o'clock, that they were, at once, to withdraw their troops from Poland, a state of war will exist

Survival!

between us. I have to tell you now that no such undertaking has been received, and that consequently this country is at war with Germany.

The situation in which no word given by Germany's ruler could be trusted and no people or country could feel itself safe, has become intolerable. Now we have resolved to finish it ... May God bless you all. May He defend the right, for it is evil things we shall be fighting against – brute force, bad faith, injustice, oppression and persecution, and against them I am certain that the right will prevail.'

To the soldiers in Aldershot the news meant that the waiting was over. Bill knew, along with his mates, that the war was now official. Great was the talk in the barrack room about the British Expeditionary Force organised by those in command. Unaware of the political implications, the men believed that Viscount Gort, the newly appointed leader of the B.E.F. would, with the initial four divisions, soon sort out the German Army. Bill recalls that fear seemed to dominate the civilian population. Fear of an aerial bombardment from the German Luftwaffe was uppermost in the minds of the locals Bill met in Aldershot. The newsreels at the cinema had shown the devastation of air raids. Government plans to prevent panic and disorder, should such raids take place, were already being implemented. Some three and a half million people were moved from vulnerable towns and cities to what was hoped would be the relative safety of the countryside. Such a number included children, expectant mothers, civil servants and the handicapped. Transport was laid on as those living in the country tried to cope with this influx of people whose habits were so different from their own.

A black-out was imposed and soon the criss-cross patterns of tape on the windows was supported by black -out material which was in short supply. "Sold Out" signs appeared in shops for such items as flashlights and batteries. Regulation after regulation was formulated by the Government and enforced, not only by the police, but by Air Raid Wardens. Sandbags were filled, concrete barricades built and those who could, hoarded food. It was a difficult time

The first job for the troops was the digging of defences and continually training with what weapons were available. Orders were issued and Bill left Aldershot in November, 1939 to join a cargo ship docked in Southampton. Packed like sardines the troops stood in ranks as the ship set sail. Rumours were rife as the Isle of Wight receded into the distance. Bill realised that this would be his first Channel crossing but such was the congestion that little enjoyment could be had from the experience – especially as a large number had yet to find their sea legs. Arriving in Cherbourg, the unit was convinced they were there simply to make up the numbers. Bill agreed, for they had little equipment to repel any sustained attack by the Germans. However, 'orders were orders' as the troops boarded a train for Caen.

Unknown to Bill and his comrades, the famed French Maginot Line fortifications extended to the west only as far as Sedan. This left some one hundred and fifty miles from Sedan to the coast unprotected. It was towards this area that the unit made its way. Allocated to a lorry and with a machine gun for company, the unit continued to travel eastwards. All were new experiences as Bill absorbed the atmosphere of the French countryside.

Christmas 1939 was celebrated with a French family who seemed poorer than those in the Shankill Road. This was an experience that has lived with Bill. Language was a major barrier to communication but at least Bill had been invited to eat with a real French family. Wine flowed as lunch was served. With a triumphant smile the farmer's wife placed the head and neck of a cockerel on Bill's plate. Two eyes stared from the head and Bill recalls moving it constantly round the plate until it was eventually taken away amid much mutterings. It was his first experience of a meal in a French home. The rest of the stay was spent in toasting France, Ireland and any country that came to mind. He returned to his unit a little unsteady on his feet and very uncertain of his future.

The winter of 1939/40 was noted for its snow, wind, frost, ice, rain and its intense cold. Thousands of old people died from the cold weather as the war in Europe began and the Germans continued their advance. Sleeping either in stables or church halls alive with mice, Bill and his comrades listened as the noise of war grew steadily louder. He recalls the sight of thousands of refugees trundling along roads jammed with farm carts, prams, lorries, military vehicles and a conglomeration of transport which showed the ingenuity of the human mind. Children too tired to walk slumped in the arms of their parents while the elderly struggled to keep pace. A look of fear and despair on the faces of those that fled as they attempted to escape from the pursuing German armies is etched into Bill's memory. Time and time again the roads suddenly emptied as the German dive-bombers and fighters machine-gunned and bombed those who sought to escape. The only shelter available when such attacks took place was in the woods and surrounding fields. The screams of the injured added to the screams of those whose nerves were shattered. Above all Bill remembers the smell of rotting animal flesh and burning buildings. It was unnerving to the young soldiers who were there to prevent such atrocities.

Yet behind the masses seeking shelter the war seemed to have had little effect. On one occasion Bill and a friend were invited to a cock fight which had been organised by the local farmers of La Basle and was held in a barn. A ring had been marked out and each cock fitted with spurs.

Bets were still being placed as the birds were let loose. With wings outstretched and talons poised the birds went for one another at a furious rate. The noise from the crowd surpassed the crows of the victorious cock as he trampled on his victim. It was to do him little good for within seconds of striking such a pose all hell broke out as bets were dishonoured. A swift withdrawal was executed as Bill and his companion edged to the barn door and finally to their billet.

Ordered to keep a look out for German paratroopers, Bill and his fellow soldiers moved slowly from billet to billet. The refugees with their lamentable possessions continued to clog the roads. The route took Bill through Caen, then Rouen. For a while he was an occupant of some First World War trenches at Arras and Vimy Ridge. This was an eerie experience, for Bill's thoughts turned to his father who had served in that war. The older men of the unit tried to calm their fears. Songs that Bill's father had sung in the First World War could be heard. Bill and his companions joined in such sing-a-longs and as he heard 'Pack up your troubles in your old kit bag' or 'It's a long way to Tipperary' he and his mates continued to have hope. At Arras reinforcements in the shape of tanks were awaited. It was now mid-May and to stem the German advance a counter-attack was proposed. Under General Martel the British Tanks advanced. Facing them was a man whose name was to figure largely in future battles – Major Erwin Rommel who commanded the 7th Panzer Division. The battle of Arras was about to begin as Mark 1 tanks, known affectionately as Matildas, faced the advancing Germans. The British tanks were slow and ponderous and, although well armoured, were poorly armed. It proved a short-lived battle and Bill and his Territorial companions felt like film extras with their small arms equipment and could only gaze in wonder as the battle raged. The German planes screeched overhead dropping bombs and firing indiscriminately. Bill witnessed the destruction of the Town Hall. The appearance of the 'real army' resulted in Bill and his companions being ordered to get to Dunkirk under their own steam.

It was now the 22nd May as Bill joined the 'useless souls' en route to Dunkirk. The journey was not without incidents. Sleeping in the cellars of bombed houses, scrounging what food and drink they could, the unit struggled towards the coast. Sheltering wherever he felt safe, Bill slept where he could. His most unusual billet on this retreat was in an undertakers house. His companion that night was a body laid out in a coffin. Drunken soldiers added to the panic as the smoke and noise increased. Danger came, not only from the air but from officers waving pistols at the men, firing indiscriminately and shouting, 'Remember we are here to die for England.' It was a worrying time and for a while it seemed that discipline had broken down.

Told to throw away everything but their rifle and destroy what they could, the Territorials witnessed the first signs of what would be known as the evacuation from Dunkirk. Footsore and weary, Bill gazed at the beach, sand dunes and ships of various shapes and sizes off-shore as well as hundreds and hundreds of men. Oil dumps on fire sent plumes of oily black smoke into the air. Several of the ships were on fire as those on board scrambled to the beach. The sand dunes gave what protection they could as members of the unit sought shelter. Exhausted, hungry, unshaven and unwashed, Bill Johnston tried to come to terms with this new predicament. He noticed that in spite of the seeming chaos there was a sense of order as groups of men were shepherded to the waiting ships.

Conversation was nigh impossible as the German Luftwaffe continued to harass the waiting troops below. A cheer would arise when the R.A.F. Spitfires retaliated. Rumours abounded but when the evacuation from Dunkirk became official the waiting, waiting, waiting, seemed interminable. Fortunately Dunkirk has a fifteen foot tide which meant that at low tide the water is shallow for a considerable distance. Queue after queue of waiting men edged their way to the ships. Overhead the enemy strafed those who waited, as slowly the smaller boats which defied description were filled with men. Once full they would make their way to the large ships which were waiting off shore. Yet success frequently evaded them as bombs exploded alongside their ships. Bill was about to board such a vessel when the force of an exploding bomb flung him into the sea. His luck held as willing hands plucked him from the sea and on board a waiting destroyer. Slumping on the deck he remembers little of the crossing to Dover but he does remember the heroism of the many sailors and soldiers who worked tirelessly for those who were marooned.

Chapter Three

Along with thousands of others Bill Johnston became, for a while, a semi-hero. Having managed to escape from Dunkirk was a feat in itself. Yet he knew, as did his comrades, that many thousands of others had yet to find sanctuary. That they did so during the days that followed seemed to Bill to be a miracle. Hundreds of extra trains had been organised to get those who had returned, away from the southern parts of England. Clearly shaken by what they saw and heard, the local population gritted their teeth as they awaited the German invasion. Meanwhile there were more pressing demands as thousands of sandwiches and mugs of tea were prepared and handed to those who had come from Dunkirk. The mix of nationalities, English, French, Polish, Belgian and Dutch, streamed in increasing numbers across the Channel. Bill remembers with gratitude those who thrust a sandwich into his hand as the train chugged its way out of the station. He did not know where he was going or why. Soon, like his companions, Bill fell asleep.

The jolting of the train as it drew to a halt resulted in heads being thrust out of windows and shouts from those N.C.O's waiting on a platform for those on board to 'Get lined up!' Stumbling from his carriage Bill joined the jostling men. Ranks were formed and the rumour spread that they were in Redruth in Cornwall. And so it proved as those in charge escorted them to Redruth Rugby Football Club.

Bill learnt that the political situation in the United Kingdom had changed. Winston Churchill was now Prime Minister and also leader of a war-time Cabinet. Bill listened to Churchill's rallying cry to the nation that, 'We shall fight on the beaches, we shall fight on the landing grounds, we shall fight in the fields and in the streets, we shall fight in the hills, we shall never surrender, and even if, which I do not for a moment believe, this island or a large part of it were subjugated and starving, then our Empire beyond the seas, armed and guarded by the British Fleet, would carry on the struggle, until, in God's good time, the

New World, with all its power and might steps forth to the rescue and liberation of the Old.' Certainly from what he heard and observed Bill realised that life had already changed. Food and clothes rationing were already in force and on the 30th May, 1940 the Government issued a further directive that 'no person shall display or cause or permit to be displayed any sign which furnishes any indication of the name of, or the situation or the direction of, or the distance to any place.' The Government directive meant the immediate removal of road signs, railway station names were painted out and buses showed no destination. It proved a worrying time, not only for Bill and his companions, but for the civilian population. The threat of an invasion by the German forces became a real factor in everyone's lives.

The people of Redruth cossetted Bill and his friend for four weeks. The army re-imposed its discipline as the memories of Dunkirk faded. Bill's unit was reminded time and time again of Churchill's words when he spoke to the House of Commons that, We must be very careful not to assign to this deliverance (Dunkirk) the attributes of victory – wars are not won by evacuations'.

Ordered to pack his kit bag, Bill was on the move again. His time at Redruth was over and he was posted to Camborne, still in the county of Cornwall. Here Bill spent a great deal of his leisure walking and generally getting fit. Living in tents under the warmth of the Cornish sun, Bill's unit rested. The joy of regular meals, being able to laugh and joke with his fellow soldiers was a bonus. However, in spite of the brave political talk, the winning of the war seemed a long way off. The Allied armies left in France after Dunkirk fought on. Paris was occupied by the Germans and a new French Government under Petain was formed. On the 17th June, 1940 the Government of France sought an armistice with Germany. On the same afternoon Churchill spoke to the nation saying, 'Whatever has happened in France makes no difference to our action and purpose. We shall do our best to be worthy of this high honour. We shall defend our island home, and with the British Empire we shall fight on, unconquerable until the curse of Hitler is lifted from the brows of mankind. We are sure that in the end all will come right.'

Thousands of troops of the once proud British Expeditionary Force had been taken into captivity but once again Bill Johnston had been lucky.

Under orders yet again, Bill departed Camborne and headed for Kingsworthy near Winchester in Hampshire. It was a journey Bill remembers for its lack of normality. Stations which bore no names (removed for security reasons) were thronged with servicemen and women of all nationalities. There was little comfort either on the stations or in the trains themselves. The light bulbs in the carriages had been painted blue while posters advertising holiday resorts had either been removed or replaced by Government posters reminding those who travelled that 'Careless talk costs lives' and 'Is your journey really necessary?' Bill was grateful for a cup of tea from a W.V.S. (Women's Voluntary Service) trolley.

Kingsworthy was headquarters and as such discipline was much stricter. Dunkirk was history. There were other battles to be fought. It was at Kingsworthy that the unit was issued with new uniforms which bore the arm badge of the Red Hand of Ulster on a khaki rectangle. Such a symbol, Bill was told, would reinforce their roots with Ireland. At Kingsworthy re-training and re-equipping began. The former left no doubt in Bill's mind that electronics would figure largely in the war.

The Germans began to intensify their bombing missions over England. Having defeated France and the Low Countries the distance flown by the Luftwaffe lessened as they began to use the aerodromes of the conquered nations. Bill was told that the Germans were dropping a mixture of bombs from their planes. Such missiles included land mines, sea mines, high explosive bombs and incendiaries, the latter containing explosive charges.

An invasion by German forces was expected at any time. The main threat it was believed, would come from the air and be followed by parachutists and a landing on the South coast. A system referred to as 'radio location' which was later changed to radar, became for a time, the first line of coastal defence. This system enabled enemy planes to be detected at some distance from the coast of England. As a result of this early warning system fighter stations and other defences could be alerted. The Observer Corps would reinforce the radar system. With a grid map, height estimator and telephone, members this Corps would relay information to Fighter Group Headquarters.

Not only were those who flew Spitfires and Hurricanes alerted, but units operating anti-aircraft guns, balloon sites and searchlights. Thus it was hoped to repulse the Luftwaffe and to make life difficult for those that flew the German 'planes As the German aerial offensive intensified, Bill's battery was posted to the South coast. Each site, whether it was for guns, balloons or searchlights was chosen to give maximum use of equipment. Such sites could be many miles away from the nearest habitation. Other sites could be placed much nearer vulnerable targets. Each site was generally self-contained, with its own water and electricity supply, tents or huts, cook-house and telephone system. Such self-containment did not happen instantly and on some occasions Bill found himself in billets – these he found much superior.

Bill's unit would be ordered to a specific site. Transport consisted of an Army lorry containing various items of equipment and capable of towing the searchlight. If things had gone according to plan, and they often didn't, the do-it-yourself huts would be there waiting. However, the most important task was to secure the searchlight. Once this had been done attention could then be focused on erecting the flimsy huts, never an easy job and often made worse by the weather. Bill remembers the intense cold and the almost constant desire to seek the warmth of the stove. Not every neighbourhood made the unit welcome. Many farmers and villagers believed that by having a searchlight unit near them, they themselves would become an easy target for the German bombers. Searchlight drill was not the only factor the members of the unit had to absorb. Arms drill, physical training, aircraft recognition, cooking and camouflaging the site left little time for leisure. Any leisure time was spent writing letters, keeping clean, attending a rare concert party or, if not too far away, visiting a pub, if one could be found open.

It was now August 1940 and Bill was posted to a searchlight unit two miles north of Portsmouth. The Battle of Britain was raging as the airfields on the South coast became the front line. Those on the ground saw heroic deeds performed by those who flew Spitfires and Hurricanes. Not only were they spectators, but in many cases victims as well as planes from both sides, having been shot down, scattered their debris over the unit. Radar defences, the eyes and ears of those who defended the country, became more and more vulnerable. As the air battle continued, Portsmouth and Southampton became targets for the German bombers. For the umpteenth time Bill came under enemy fire.

On duty with the ack-ack. Bill seated far left.

Bill off duty.

Some two to three hundred German bombers, escorted by fighters, would wing their way across the Channel. To protect targets from such attacks the country was divided into one hundred and thirty areas which were, at the time, based on the layout of the national telephone system. When the enemy aircraft were some twenty miles from the coast a yellow warning light would be flashed to the units. Five minutes later this would be changed to a red alert and when the enemy aircraft passed overhead a green warning was issued. Thus radar and the Royal Observer Corps gave as much warning as was technically possible at that time to those who were defending the country. Bill's role in his searchlight unit was that of sound locator. Above the noise of the 'planes, bombs and guns Bill's team would track the raiders. The information they gathered would be passed to those who operated the searchlight. At night, decisions then had to be made as to the timing of the light and the distance it was to be projected. Sweeping the sky at night the light might cone a German 'plane. Other searchlights would add to the cone and the battle would begin. Frequently R.A.F. fighters would join the fray. Bill recalls a letter of thanks from Cat's Eye Cunningham, a famous fighter ace, after he had successfully shot down a German raider. A letter like this was a boost to morale. Another morale booster was when the unit, by use of the searchlight, shepherded R.A.F. 'planes back to base. As a result of his work Bill was promoted to Lance Corporal.

Two incidents stand out in Bill's memory during his tour of duty on the south coast. One was the number of men, women and children who trudged from the cities to the countryside seeking shelter from the German aerial onslaught. This was hardly surprising, for Portsmouth was a naval dockyard of some importance. What happened in Portsmouth also gave an indication of what was happening to other cities up and down the country. Portsmouth suffered major attacks. Public buildings, churches, factories, schools, cinemas, shops and homes were destroyed. Not only were high explosive bombs used on the city but also incendiaries and parachute mines – the latter a major cause of destruction. A Mass Observation report in February 1941 spoke of Portsmouth as a 'tomb of darkness'. Portsmouth and Southampton became depressing places to visit as the rubble mounted from demolished factories, shops and houses. Bill compared the destruction to that which he had witnessed with the British Expeditionary Force. The other incident concerned a replacement who had joined the unit. After tasting the rations the unit were supplied with he volunteered for the duty of cook. However there was a condition attached. The new member, prior to his enlistment, owned a café in Soho, London. On condition that the men would contribute two shillings and sixpence each every week he would cook.

There were some who grumbled but the majority agreed to go along with this innovation. No questions were asked as to how or where the additional food was purchased but all agreed it was a great improvement. Their joy was short-lived for the officers heard of the cook's ability and he was whisked off to the nearest Officer's Mess.

In spite of the bombing Bill's luck held. Not all were so lucky for a number of anti-aircraft personnel were killed or wounded. Moving along the coast the searchlight unit continued on full alert. Rations, including fuel for the stove had a habit of being late or not turning up at all. Still the raids by Heinkels, Junkers and Dorniers followed, day by day, night after night. It was a critical time as the R.A.F. and other defences mounted counter-attack after counter-attack. As the Germans switched targets to other industrialised areas Bill realised he had little responsibility for his own destiny.

Perhaps the incident which made Bill think that a change of direction was necessary was a proposed visit by royalty. Suddenly all hell broke loose. Huts were inspected, kit was laid out, sheets and pillowcases were issued and special food was prepared. The royal visit never materialised and all luxuries were taken back to whence they came. Now at Marlborough, Bill read a notice that the Royal Navy were recruiting gunners, and the R.A.F, aircrew. Serving Territorials were invited to apply.

Chapter Four

Bill Johnston's response to the plea for aircrew was not immediate. His thoughts lingered on his current role and his recent experiences of watching the R.A.F. in action. The possibility of applying for a post as a gunner on board a ship did not appeal. A decision had to be made.

Bill had read the extracts from Winston Churchill's speech when he spoke on the 20th of August. He recalled that 'The gratitude of every home in our island, in our Empire, and indeed throughout the world, goes out to the British airmen who, undaunted by odds, unwearied in their constant challenge and mortal danger, are turning the tide of the World War by their prowess and by their devotion. Never in the field of human conflict was so much owed by so many to so few.'

Bill had seen such heroism with his own eyes and decided that he would apply to the R.A.F. as potential air crew. He was the only soldier in his unit to do so. Seeking approval for his application to be processed took little time. What took the time was the response to that application.

Eventually Bill was ordered to Stratford-on-Avon in Warwickshire. Told to report to the Shakespeare Hotel he found himself in another world. The Shakespeare Hotel, famed as a meeting place for actors and critics, was, during this period of the war, host to the military. On reporting, Bill was detailed to a room shared with others who wished to join aircrew. He was ordered to be at the Stratford Theatre at 09.00 hours the following morning.

Stratford-on-Avon, famous as the birthplace of William Shakespeare, was, like all towns and cities during the war, beset with problems. The blackout was a major hurdle for any 'visitor' to overcome. Those who were to take an examination for admission to the Royal Air Force were circumspect, and rather than explore the town by blundering round the darkened streets, spent their first night discussing the likely questions of the first examination. The first exam was of an educational nature and was followed next day by a medical. Bill felt confident that he had not disgraced himself in either examination but no results were given and he returned to duty with the searchlight unit.

Within a few weeks Bill was informed that he had been successful in both examinations and was again under orders. The Royal Air Force was desperately short of aircrew. The Battle of Britain, so recently won, had been at a cost of both men and machines. Men were needed to train not only for fighters but also for bombers and such training took time.

On the 3rd of September 1940 Winston Churchill had said, 'The fighters are our salvation, but the bombers alone provide the means of victory. We must therefore develop the power to carry an ever-increasing volume of explosives to Germany, so as to pulverise the entire industry and scientific structure on which the war effort and economic life of the enemy depend, while holding him at arm's length from our island.'

Exchanging his army uniform for the blue of the R.A.F. he was given a railway warrant to Scarborough in the North Riding of Yorkshire. Scarborough, an east coast holiday resort noted for its beaches, hotels and seaside atmosphere was full of military personnel. Not quite the Blackpool Bill had dreamed of as a boy but an exciting posting, even in the blackout. On Bill's forage cap there now appeared a white flash, which indicated that he was attending an Initial Training Wing Course, and he was promoted to Leading Aircraftsman. The resultant pay increase proved of value.

Bill quickly learnt that the ranks of the R.A.F. were different from the army. He soon added to his vocabulary such words as Flight Lieutenant, Squadron Leader and Wing Commander, although he found that the discipline he was experiencing now was less harsh than that of the army. Billeted in the Crown Hotel, he found himself in a room filled with six iron bedsteads. Biscuit mattresses, sheets and blankets were issued, as Bill gave a wry smile when he recalled his army experience with sheets. Exploring his new surroundings he found a room converted to a gym with weight-lifting equipment and boxing gloves. There were also facilities for table tennis and billiards. A schedule of lectures was issued, for as the officer said, 'It will be nose to the grindstone for six weeks.'

Scarborough on a fine summer day can be a splendid place. It was now mid-1941, the sun shone but those hoping to further their training had little time to enjoy the resort's wartime pleasures. Lectures were held at the imposing Grand Hotel and it was to this venue that they were marched every day. Books were issued with the strict instruction that they were to be handed back on completion of the course.

The rudiments of aircraft recognition, theory of flight, armaments, meteorology, astronomy, navigation, instruments, Morse code, aero engines and photography were explained. Problems were set and had to be solved and a smattering of R.A.F. law was included. Bill found some lectures more interesting than others. Still there were no half measures for to progress one had to succeed at every subject. The physical aspect of those on the course was not neglected. As well as marching to and from lectures the Leading Aircraftsmen were expected to attend physical training on the beach and to undertake guard duty. Not all did so for there was work to catch up on or a girl friend to meet.

On the few occasions that Bill went into town it was to enjoy a visit to the cinema or to sample a plate of egg and chips in a local café. There was also the odd concert party and now and again an invitation into a local's home. All on the course were reminded that if they demonstrated aptitude and ability success should follow. Not all lecturers were good at passing on information. Those with a monotonous voice and lack of interest were the worst. Many of the lectures were given by ex-Grammar school teachers. These were men who a few months before had taught in the sixth form and a number on the Initial Training Wing had just left such sixth forms. The better ones introduced competition and fun into their lectures. Practising Morse code by key and light proved a test, not only for memory but also for dexterity. The instructor would flash out the code number of an imaginary aerodrome to which the students would respond with a recognition signal. Many a laugh was enjoyed as the Morse code was misinterpreted. Why R.A.F. law was part of the programme remains a mystery. Bill recalls that under such law an R.A.F. officer could not be prosecuted in the civil courts for a debt of less than £30 – an enormous sum to the Irishman from the Shankill Road. He also remembers, as exams loomed, the Flight Commander saying, 'It's no good refreshing your memory with questions you're not going to get!'

Success on the Initial Training Wing course at Scarborough meant a forty-eight hour pass. Not so for Bill Johnston. His home town was Belfast. This, coupled with the difficulty of travelling in wartime, resulted in Bill being granted a seventy two hour pass. Good-byes were said and Bill headed for the Shankill Road. This was his first appearance in the 'Road' in his R.A.F. uniform and as someone who was hopefully training for air crew he was treated with respect. His actual stay in the city was limited as most of the seventy two hours was taken up with the journey. Still, being able to see members of his family made a difference.

Shankill Road had changed little. The hatred between Catholics and Protestants continued and there was evidence of such hatred in the attacks on people and their homes. Belfast had been bombed. The Harland and Wolfe shipyards, together with the aircraft factories, had suffered from the bombing and also from the fires caused by the incendiaries. The fires had spread quickly, causing widespread devastation. The anti-aircraft defences had proved inadequate, as had the shelters for the civilian population. Houses, factories and many commercial premises were destroyed. The experiences of those in Belfast who suffered from the German blitz resulted in many seeking shelter in the countryside. These people were known as 'ditchers'.

Temporary huts were erected on open spaces to be used as accommodation for those who had been bombed out. Intolerance continued but at least there was more work about as the factories and dockyards stepped up production to meet the demands of war.

Bill found that he missed the youthful company of the Training Wing and after the dutiful visits to relatives he headed back to Scarborough. His joy was short -lived for on his return he discovered that those who had a forty-eight hour pass had already been posted. However he was not downcast for long, when told that he would be on the next draft out bound for America.

Further enquiries revealed that Bill was to be considered as a candidate for air -crew under the Arnold Scheme. America, not yet in the war, had agreed to organise four training schemes – the others were the B.F.T.S. Scheme, (Basic Flying Training), the Pan-American Airways Observers School and the Towers Scheme. At the time these were new initiatives. The Arnold Scheme meant American military discipline but flying tuition would be carried out by civilian instructors.

Excited by the prospect of further travel, Bill was issued with some rather smart American clothing. This would, it was believed, not embarrass the United States authorities and give a sense of belonging to those who joined the Arnold Scheme. Slowly but surely enough personnel were being gathered to justify a journey across the Atlantic, a hazardous journey in 1941 as German submarines lurked beneath the waves, waiting to pounce on Allied shipping.

The German U-boats had already established the reputation of a force to be reckoned with. At the outbreak of war the German submarine U-30 had torpedoed the Athenia, a British liner with some 1,103 passengers on board. One hundred and twelve lost their lives. This was quickly followed by the sinking of the aircraft carrier H.M.S. Courageous in the Atlantic Ocean. The losses, not only in well-armed ships but also in merchant shipping, continued. Bill and his companions, as well as the Captain and ship's crew knew that a journey by ship across the Atlantic was perilous.

Ordered to report to Greenock on the Firth of Clyde Bill, along with hundreds of other potential air crew, boarded a Union Castle liner. Bill's dream of a luxury cruise was dented when he was taken down to the hold of the ship and presented with a hammock and blankets. At night the hammocks were strung up over the dining tables. Getting used to this new form of 'bed' took a little time. Conditions were cramped although generally they had the run of the liner. They were told where to eat, to undertake lifeboat drill and what, if any, duties were to be performed. Beneath the babble of conversation there was a certain disquiet. All knew that the ship's speed was her best defence. None knew what lay ahead as the liner slipped its moorings and headed for the Atlantic.

Bill remembers little of the crossing. Always a good sailor he did not suffer, as did others, from the dreaded sea-sickness. Once, thoughtlessly, he accepted a place in a card school. His Protestant upbringing had not prepared him for such a school, so he was taken to the cleaners by those with more skill than he possessed. However, he listened and learned from those on board. Such hopes and dreams surfaced from those on board that, at times, Bill was bewildered. The talk of the potential air crew was not only about flying but about the Americas. They had been reminded on countless occasions that they were ambassadors of the Royal Air Force and that brought not only privileges but responsibilities.

The crossing proved uneventful. Newfoundland appeared out of the fog. Halifax, set in the rocky coastline with small hills in the background, reminded Bill of Scotland. All was new yet nothing was new as Bill recalled tales from his childhood of Irish immigrants setting forth seeking a new life. That he had several advantages over such immigrants he did not deny. The crossing had been paid for by the government together with his food and clothing. Admittedly he was not free but he had found the company of his young companions stimulating. Once the formalities of docking had been accomplished the trainee aircrew disembarked and awaited orders. From the dockside to the railway station they travelled to be told that their journey would continue by train following the St. Lawrence river passing Quebec, Montreal and on to Toronto. Bill could think of no better introduction to Canada.

Toronto proved to be yet another holding post. Such posts were becoming a familiar stopping place and were used to ensure that sufficient personnel were gathered together to make the next stage of the journey viable. When Bill arrived, not enough personnel had been assembled to justify further transit. During this period of waiting Bill, along with some of his companions, took the opportunity of exploring the surrounding area. One such visit he vividly recalls. This was to Niagara Falls and his first introduction to the United States of America. Boarding a Greyhound bus Bill travelled to see this wondrous sight. Long before he saw the three-hundred-foot falls he was aware of the noise and the moisture-laden air. He watched in awe as steamboats took tourists to the foot of the Falls All were equipped with raincoats but Bill did not emulate them. Hitching a lift back to camp presented no problems as Bill and his friends were dropped outside the camp gates. Bill also visited Timothy Eaton's Store. Eaton was famous for helping Irish immigrants as they struggled to establish a new life in a new world. Bill took this opportunity to send home a food parcel which was gratefully received.

Sleeping accommodation at this time varied depending upon what stage you arrived at the transit camp. In Bill's case it was in stables while others bedded down in sheds. He recalls that it was Ontario State Show Week which provided grand entertainment of a nature he had not seen before. This was Bill's first experience of a Rodeo. He witnessed what he had only seen on the cinema screen previously – bucking broncos, cowboys lassoing cattle, feats of rope-spinning and bare back riding. However he was reassured by the sight and noise of a fun fair and decided that such fairs were the same the world over. Each experience added to Bill's knowledge of this vast and varied country.

Eventually enough personnel were assembled to enable Bill Johnston to travel, under Government orders, into America. His destination, the State of Georgia. Bill had already completed a train journey of over five hundred miles but the proposed trip would far exceed this. Once again Bill, along with others, boarded a train which was to be their home for the next few days. American trains, he had discovered, were better equipped and furnished and much more luxurious than their British counterparts. Sleek and well-built American trains were, in Bill's eyes, the ideal way to travel. Rather than the cramped conditions of British trains he found that the train he had boarded lacked for nothing in the way of luxuries. Spacious seats, ingenious sleeping accommodation and wash rooms, air conditioning, a restaurant car that served some of the best food he had ever tasted and stewards who seemed to anticipate every need. The days of the future young aircrew were spent chatting, playing cards, reading, sleeping or gazing and commenting on the ever-changing landscape. It was a journey that etched itself into the mind of the young Irishman and made him wonder why he seemed to be so lucky.

The journey from Toronto to Albany in Georgia covered some eleven hundred miles of track. Passing through Michigan, Ohio, Kentucky and Tennessee, Bill was fascinated with such names as Nashville, Chattanooga and Atlanta. Gazing from the window of the speeding train he could only wonder at the size of the United States and the variety of the townships. Industrialisation gave way to more cultivated, open land until the train finally arrived at its destination. Stepping down from the train Bill was, in spite of his light American clothing, struck with the humidity and the heat. However he had little time to stand and stare as transport took him to his next destination.

Student pilots. Paddy seated second left.

Instructors (crop dusters) at Darr - Tech.

Survival!

Chapter Five

So Albany it was. Well, not exactly Albany but Darr – Aero Tech a few miles out of town. Darr – Aero Tech, a civilian flying school, founded by H. S. Darr, was one of the six 'Primary Schools' under the Arnold Scheme. Here Bill, along with one hundred and thirteen other flying cadets would undergo an initial training course. They were known as Class 42C and their liaison officer was Flight Lieutenant Hill of the R.A.F.

During the autumn of 1941 Darr -Tech was slowly becoming conscious of its role. The aerodrome was a grass field of some acreage bordered by buildings, parade ground and an administration block. The cadets were a mixed bag of personalities which had yet to gel. Some cadets could claim as their birthright to being born a Scot, others Irish, some Welsh while others claimed Yorkshire or Devon as their place of birth. The youngest was eighteen. A number, while on the course, would celebrate their twenty-first birthdays. It was rumoured that there was even an elder statesman of thirty-one years in the intake. Their careers to date had spanned many disciplines. Farmers, accountants, clerks, civil servants were but a few of their diverse beginnings. Nicknames abounded. Although he was not the only Irishman on the course Bill was to become Paddy. Other nicknames beggar belief, for ask where Colossus, Chips, Casanova, Pitch or Ace were and from somewhere there would be a response.

Darr -Tech was to be Paddy-s home for the next two months. This out-of-town airfield was administered by the United States Army Air Corps. It was the U.S.A.A.F. that would provide accommodation, food, and discipline while civilian instructors would provide lessons in flying skills. Such instructors were in the main, young men who were known as 'crop dusters'. The Southern states of America had huge areas of land under cultivation Such land produced, as a result of careful husbandry, large quantities of food. The crops grown required constant attention.

Part of that attention was the spraying of chemicals at certain times of the year on to the crop to prevent the build-up of pests and diseases. This spraying, or dusting, was undertaken by 'crop dusters'. When not involved in agricultural work the 'crop dusters' would be working in a flying circus or flying people and goods out to distant places. To Bill Johnston it seemed a splendid way to earn a living. However, the forty-one 'crop dusters' at Darr - Aero Tech were now employed to teach the rudiments of flying to those who had shown potential as possible air crew.

To Paddy Johnston the initial introduction to the course did not augur well. As he and the other cadets stood at ease while being addressed by a senior officer he listened with some trepidation. The words 'Look to your left, look to your right,' echoed in their ears. Having done so they were then told that two out of three people would fail the course. However, the voice continued, 'Those of you who do not make the initial grade of pilot may qualify in other aspects of aircrew.' This was scant consolation to young Paddy who now believed he was a born fighter pilot.

The planes they would be taught to fly were Stearmans. These were hardy and reliable two seater biplanes with a maximum speed of one hundred and twenty five miles per hour and a range of some five hundred miles. Following the Battle of Britain many believed that the war against Germany would be won by the country that possessed the most powerful air force. The losses of pilots, navigators, air gunners and bomb-aimers meant that there was a continual drain on such resources. It was the task of places like Darr - Aero Tech to replace such personnel. Flying cadets were expected to go solo after eight hours of instruction. Competition among the four flights was encouraged as the 'crop dusters' sought out the potential pilots.

The role of the U.S.A.A.F. in the 6th Albany scheme included drill, guard duty, some details about the U. S. A., in particular Georgia, as well as all the usual callisthenics. Meals were served by coloured stewards and food such as Paddy had never tasted. At one stage the cadets requested less, for the chef's expectation of their appetites was such that food was being wasted. This was a cause to support but not in America.

The blue skies over Georgia meant that flying instruction began early, sometimes as early as five o'clock. Initially the instructors would be referred to as 'mister'. Their role at Darr – Aero Tech was to pass on to the Flying Cadets the knowledge and skill of flying. The majority did this with patience and tact. As the cadets became familiar with the stick, rudder and switches of the Stearman so their confidence grew although at times there were fatalities. Not only did they have to understand the workings of the plane but they also had to remember local landmarks as

Survival!

day after day circuits and bumps were practised. Occasionally flying would be postponed as a hurricane was forecast but probably the greatest danger, Paddy recalls, was that of other Stearmans bouncing along the hundred and fifty foot grass strip. Wearing a leather helmet and goggles the cadets would be taken through the basic rules of flying. How to take off, land, turn. All Stearmans had fixed undercarriages yet all, according to Paddy, were capable of a life of their own. Some instructors came to believe that certain cadets believed they were taking off when, in fact, they were landing. However as time progressed relationships were built up and confidence grew. Paddy soloed after eight hours and was pleased with his progress.

The sergeant taking drill was not so pleased. The U.S.A.A.F. had a different philosophy to drill from the R.A.F. There was no such order as right or left turn. Instead it was 'left face, right face.' You were expected to be better than the man next to you. Hazing had long been an acceptable and routine method of discipline with the United States Army. The cadets, away from the instructors, were exposed to a harsh hierarchical authority. Lights out was at ten o'clock and anyone found talking after that time was given a demerit. Other demerits were given for failure to salute an officer or the American flag. Paddy recalls that mealtimes could be a demerit heaven for they were awarded for using the cruet without permission or talking too loudly. Punishment would entail marching round the square wearing full kit and saluting the flag each time, being confined to camp or given some domestic chore. He remembers a time on the parade ground when the sergeant screamed at him, (he was no more than six inches away), 'What are you famous for?'

Paddy had suffered harassment from this sergeant and his response was instant. He was 'the flyweight champion of Ireland.' Startled, the sergeant nodded, stepped back and moved on to his next victim. While at Darr – Aero Tech Paddy became famous as a boxing champion. His luck held, for he never had to defend his mythical title, and the 'hazing' ceased.

Life was not all work. Georgia and Darr – Tech seemed an idyllic time not only for the sunshine, fresh air and food but also for the companionship of others. On the base some cadets formed a Glee Club, others played tennis, cards or chess while others swam. Those cadets who were married, and there were a number, spent hours writing letters and hanging round the mail-box. Many listened to swing music and tried jitterbugging. Not all activities took place on the aerodrome. Albany had its bowling lanes in North Washington Street, its 'Dining and Dancing' at the Hangar Club. There was also the Rialto Pool Room, the Royal Ice Cream Parlor along with ice skating and the cinema. The bus service to such new leisure activities was good. On one trip back to camp Paddy was offered a lift by a negro and as it was raining it was one he gladly accepted. Dropped outside the gate he thanked the driver and thought how kind folk were. The next day Paddy was called to give an account of his behaviour. Shocked, he simply stated that he had not been brought up in a culture of apartheid. Given a dressing down, he was reminded with some force, that such a culture did exist in Georgia and while undergoing training Flying Cadet Johnston must understand and respect such a culture.

Paddy, on reflection, was not sure which was worse – the culture of Georgia or that of the Shankill Road. The population of the former was some seventy per cent negro and thirty per cent white, yet white dominated. On the buses the whites sat in the front and the blacks in the back. There was segregation on the sidewalks, the parks and the graveyards. In fact every aspect of Georgian life was dominated by colour, even education. With its cotton and tobacco plantations it presented a face of prosperity but in Paddy's mind underlaid with intolerance similar to that he had known as a boy.

The notice board was one of the main sources of information concerning life at Darr - Aero Tech. Here would be posted which in-structor was flying with which cadet and who had soloed successfully. Other official notices appeared, alongside telephone numbers of families who would entertain the cadets for a day or a weekend. Contact would be made by telephone and a car would arrive at the base to pickup the intrepid cadets. Many of the families who did this had daughters who were home from college and wished to fill their date books. These young ladies were known as 'Georgian Peaches' and would collect cadets as a boy would collect stamps. Still the hospitality was unlike anything Paddy had experienced. Parties and dances would be arranged and trips to the countryside organised where Coke would be drunk and if the fancy took them the couples would dance to the music of the juke box. Photographs were exchanged and occasionally a serious relationship developed.

Paddy would listen to tales the ladies would recount of the great estates their great grand-daddy had owned prior to the Civil War. Certainly those in power lived well. As Paddy remarked, 'The young ladies of Georgia knew how to handle men, but it was good to be king for a day.'

However, the Government's purpose in sending them to the States was to train them as aircrew, especially pilots. Paddy soloed within the allotted time and was posted to Macon for yet another course. He was not alone.

Once again Paddy realised that friendships formed in wartime were ephemeral.

Chapter Six

Paddy did not have far to travel. Some two hundred miles north of Albany in the state of Georgia lies the small township of Macon. Here, outside the town, at Cochran Field, was a Military Academy for flying cadets. The surrounding area was noted for its peaches and peanuts but Paddy found the town to his liking. Here, during his hours of leisure, he would dance, practice ice-skating and occasionally go bowling. Not that he had much time for such activities.

Cadets had come to Cochran Field from other Primary courses. Once again introductions were made while the serious business of learning to fly military aircraft began. Discipline was much stricter and to Paddy's mind, harsh. Senior cadets were sanctioned by authority to 'haze' juniors. This was interpreted as bullying by those on whom it was inflicted. Speaking at mealtimes was not allowed unless approved by a senior. Drill and physical training ensured that all nationalities on the course were fit. Not only was there instruction in the air but also in the classroom. Flying lessons were performed in Harvard 'planes. Even with three cushions under him and two behind Paddy's lack of height proved a problem. He felt uncomfortable and lost a degree of confidence. His nickname almost changed to 'five cushion Johnston' but it was a short-lived affair. However, his navigational skills, honed in the classroom and in the air, were recognised. Packing his kitbag for yet another train journey, Paddy wondered what life had in store for him, such was the sensitivity of the United States involvement in training fliers in the summer of 1941 that all documentation of his period at Darr - Tech and Cochran Field was taken from him.

Number 656566 L.A.C. William Johnston was again on the move, this time to Canada. During December 1941 the world situation changed. For some time Japan had been pressing America to lift economic sanctions which the American Government had imposed. America refused, and coded messages from the Japanese Government had been unravelled which suggested that the Japanese could launch an attack against an American base, possibly in the Philippines. On the seventh of December of that year Japanese fighters and bombers flying from aircraft carriers attacked Pearl Harbour. Enormous damage was inflicted on the American fleet which was stationed there. Many American warships were put out of action by some three hundred and sixty six Japanese bombers and fighters which had taken off from aircraft carriers. Aircraft and airfields were also destroyed and over two thousand Americans killed, not only did the Japanese use aircraft but midget submarines inflicted further destruction. Pearl Harbour was not the only place to be attacked on that infamous day, 7th of December, 1941. Attacks were also made by the Japanese against Malaya, Hong Kong and the Philippines. In all such attacks surprise and disbelief were the important elements. Roosevelt, President of the United States, declared in a message to Congress that 'No matter how long it may take us to overcome this premeditated invasion, the American people in their righteous might will win through to absolute victory.' On the eighth of December Prime Minister Winston Churchill informed the Japanese Government 'that a state of war exists between our two countries.' On the eleventh of December Germany declared war on the United States of America. The war was now global. The result of these declarations was not only an increase in aeroplane production but also an increase in the number of aircrew undergoing training.

Paddy's destination this time was Portage La Prairie, Manitoba. Boarding a train at Macon he was to undertake the longest train journey of his life. Because of the nature of the American and Canadian countryside and the railway system, he travelled East in order to go West, passing through Atlanta, Washington, Baltimore and then on to New York and Boston. At Boston he changed trains and travelled up the coast to Bangor. From Bangor the train meandered through Moncton, Bellville, Toronto, Thunder Bay and Winnipeg. Paddy found the experience fascinating. He couldn't believe he was being paid as well.

The latter part of the journey had taken Paddy around the Great Lakes. The contrast with Albany could not have been greater. Snow and ice abounded and the young cadets were warned not to touch bare metal with bare hands. They were also warned to look out for frostbite. The Royal Canadian Air Force base at Portage La Prairie was, however, well adapted to winter weather and soon Paddy was installed with yet another group of new companions.

Now that America was in the war there seemed to be a greater urgency in the training of aircrew. It was at Portage La Prairie that Paddy was issued with a new log book. The instructions on this Observers and Air Gunners Flying log book issued by the R.C.A.F. make interesting reading:

1. This log book is an official document and the property of H.M. Government.

2. Observers and air gunners will maintain an accurate and detailed record of all flights undertaken on service aircraft.

3. Proficiency assessments will be recorded on the appropriate page at the back of the book annually on 31st December, on posting or on attachment to another unit for flying duties.

4. Bombing and Air Gunnery records will be entered in the appropriate pages at the back of the book annually on 31st December.

5. Monthly totals will be entered on a single line in red ink and initialled by the Commanding Officer or his deputy.

In spite of it being the property of H.M. Government Paddy still has his log book. His first entry in a neat hand was on the 30th January, 1942. On that date at 19.25 hours he flew as an observer for two hours fifty-five minutes under the instruction of Mr. Parsons. The journey took them from Portage to Sladstone, then to Birtle and Elkhorn, past Souris and Carmen before finally returning to base. Mr. Parsons was, like the other flying instructors, a civilian.

The Observers course was a test of mental ability and communication skills. Lectures on navigational techniques were time-tabled. Other lectures concerned the role of the bomb-aimer, maps and charts, magnetism and compass work, signals, meteorology, photography, reconnaissance, armaments and bombing. The course lasted ninety-seven days and involved tests and examinations both practical and written. It was an exciting time for the young Irishman who never lost his love of flying.

Landmarks became more familiar as navigational aids, churches, roads, rivers and railway lines were the things to look out for. During February Paddy acted as navigator four times, observer twice and bomb aimer once. During this month he had seven different pilots and seven different assessments. All good! Not only were his skills improving but his flying hours were mounting up. He completed twenty hours and twenty minutes during this shortest of months.

March of 1942 witnessed Paddy utilising his photographic skills and also dropping his first practice bombs. The weather, as ever, dictated when the Anson 'planes would fly. During this period Paddy flew for six hours twenty minutes at night. All in all he seemed set fair.

It was not all work, weekends were free. This was an opportunity to catch up on letter writing, sport, dancing, listening to music and going out with girls. The news from home was not encouraging. Rationing continued to dominate everyone's life. Canned foods such as meat, fruit and vegetables were made available on a points system. This gave a much fairer distribution of food which had tended to be bought and hoarded by the better-off. Soap was also added to the points system and the white loaf began to change to a grey colour. This was due to the extraction rate of wheat being raised from seventy per cent to eighty per cent. Paddy also learned that cigarettes were in short supply as well as razor blades. Other news concerning the conflict was equally depressing, especially the loss of merchant shipping due to German U-boat action and the continuing bombing raids by the Luftwaffe. During a visit to Portage Paddy decided to send another food parcel home. Portage boasted a small Eaton's food store. Upon entering Paddy stated his requirements and the address in Ireland to which he wanted the parcel sent. The manager overheard this and engaged Paddy in conversation, stating that his wife came from Ulster. They chatted some more and Paddy received an invitation to dinner. He enjoyed an excellent meal as well as a good deal of talk about 'the old country'. Paddy told them that he was hoping to go to Winnipeg on his next weekend off. Without further ado his hostess phoned a friend in Winnipeg and gave him a letter of introduction. The letter was to a Mrs. McKaig. Paddy took his letter with him on his next visit to Winnipeg. His luck held for Mrs. McKaig and her family were waiting to entertain him. This meeting was the start of many such gatherings and developed into a friendship which was to last over the years. The McKaig family had two daughters in their last year at school and their father Jack held an important job at Eaton's store. Jack told of his early days in Belfast and showed Paddy the wooden shack that they had first lived in when they emigrated to Canada. They now lived in River Heights, a much more salubrious area and they also had a cabin at Victoria Beach. This was a place to which Paddy frequently retreated. Here were not only sandy beaches but tennis courts and some splendid walks in the woods. Paddy remembers this place with great affection for there were lots of young folk about who had a zest for life.

The course continued apace. April 1942 saw him assessed as a navigator, observer and bomb aimer under the watchful eyes of pilots, McCaw, Roberts, Espland, Mills, Black, Garsky and Faulkner. That month he clocked up twenty two hours and five minutes of flying time. Nine hours and 55minutes of that involved night flying. His final marks of the course held at No. 7 Air Observer School resulted in an overall average of 74.4% with his highest marks being in navigation. Paddy was well pleased with his progress to date.

The Royal Canadian Air Force changed tack during May. It was now the turn of their pilots to teach the skills of bombing and air gunnery to the young Irishman. This course was held at the Bombing and Gunnery School, MacDonald, Manitoba and lasted forty one days. Flying at

R.C.A.F. R.96
(R.A.F. 1767)
10M-1-42(1531)
H.Q. 1062-3-79

Certificates of Qualification

(to be filled in as appropriate)

1. This is to certify that William Johnston
has qualified as Air Observer navigator
with effect from 26 : 4 : 42 Sgd. D Riddell
Date 25 : 4 : 42 Unit 7 A.O.S.

2. This is to certify that 656566 LAC JOHNSTON. W.
has qualified as BOMB AIMER & AIR GUNNER
with effect from 8 - 6 - 42 Sgd. G W Ross
Date 5 - 6 - 42 Unit 3 B&G.

3. This is to certify that Johnston, W.
has qualified as ASTRONOMICAL NAVIGATOR
with effect from 18 - 7 - 42 Sgd. Mitchell A.
Date 30 - 7 - 42 Unit 1 CANS

4. This is to certify that
has qualified as
with effect from Sgd.
Date Unit

Night Vision Test B'Mth. 25/8/42 19/32

every opportunity when take-off times varied from 01.35 hours to 21.30 hours, Paddy made steady, if unspectacular, progress. On the sixth of June his examination result showed that he had gained 70% of the necessary marks and had passed. He also gained 74% of the marks as an air gunner flying Battle aircraft. All in all a satisfactory time for the young man from the Shankill Road.

During June and July Paddy continued to improve his skills as a navigator/observer. This was advanced navigation and the course, held at No. 1. Advanced Navigation School, Rivers, Manitoba was to be his last training exercise in Canada.

His tunic now boasted half a wing with the letter 'O' at the base. Paddy's chest expanded a little for he was proud of his success. On reflection the hardest part of the course had been that of astro-navigation. Flying at night using a sextant and the stars as aids, together with tables of calculations, Paddy was able to pinpoint the plane's position. This was a skilled science that was soon to be superseded by further electronic equipment.

The decision was made by those in command that Paddy, along with a number of his companions, was to return to the United Kingdom. He was posted to Montreal to join a crew which was to fly a new 'plane to England. For four weeks they waited and enjoyed the sights and sounds of Montreal. They waited in vain as the 'plane failed to materialise. The authorities then decided to post them to Halifax. Here they boarded a large P.&O. liner to Liverpool. Being not only sergeants now but sergeants with wings and half wings they were given cabins and had the run of the ship. On arrival at Liverpool Paddy and his companions were posted to a transit camp in Bournemouth.

Chapter Seven

Paddy had forgotten what a desperate plight the country was in. He could, during his months stay in Bournemouth, hardly believe the changes that had taken place. Bournemouth had not escaped the bombing by the German Luftwaffe and had its own quota of air raid shelters and canteens, hoardings and buildings were now sprinkled with Government posters telling people to 'carry your gas mask always,' and 'to look out in the blackout,' and 'not to waste food'. The number of posters that Paddy read made him realise that once again he was in a country fighting for survival.

Conscription for unmarried women between the ages of twenty and thirty had been introduced. The clothing ration had been cut and Paddy found it difficult to believe that civilians were rationed to one egg and one packet of dried egg per month. Certainly the more affluent people of Bournemouth seemed to have found other sources of food and clothing. He recalled his duties as a lance-corporal working on a searchlight unit some miles east of his present location and believed he had made the right decision in transferring to the R.A.F. Paddy was also more familiar than most with the influx of American troops known as G.I.'s. The initials stood for 'Government Issue' and appeared on the equipment the Americans brought with them. It became the norm to refer to the thousands of American service personnel as G.I.'s. The Americans brought with them not only equipment and money but a culture that oozed confidence. One of the major problems that local residents had to come to terms with was that of colour. The Americans operated a system of 'whites only', and 'negroes only' zones and this caused some disquiet in the pubs and inns where they spent some of their off-duty time. They also continued to be self-contained with their own films, radios and newspapers. He was also able to understand the fascination of many English girls for these brash, boastful and rich Allies. The music of Glenn Miller, Benny Goodman and Duke Ellington was perhaps the most common bond of the serving forces.

Bournemouth proved a holding post and soon the young sergeant was on his travels once again. His posting this time was to Bobbington in the Midlands. It was now September 1942 and during this month Paddy flew for nine and a half hours in Ansons, (standard trainer aircraft). During the five flights he made Paddy sharpened his skills in photography and bombing. The course he was on was an Air Bomber Advanced Course. Due to the continual demand for aircrew he did not complete the course and was posted yet again. This time it was to Number 15 Operational Training Unit at Harwell. The purpose of this posting was to 'convert' Paddy and others to the vagaries of the Wellington bomber. The Wellington was a twin-engined bomber built on the geodetic method. This was a system of metal lattices which were covered with fabric and the plane was manned by a crew of six. As with all aircraft at this time, technology was developing at a furious rate and subsequently the Wellington bomber underwent various up-dates.

Harwell airfield, like so many at this time, was an assortment of temporary buildings and concrete runways. On the 6th of November, 1942 Paddy spent five hours acting as second pilot doing circuits and bumps. This involved flying on a set route, landing, and then taking off again. The senior pilot was a Flight Sergeant. This followed the British custom that no matter what rank he held the pilot was Captain of the aircraft. The Wellington was considered by those who flew it, to be a good strong twin-engined aircraft which could cruise at 165 m.p.h. and the bomb load which could be carried totalled 4,500 lbs. The aircraft had a ceiling height of 15,000 feet.

Paddy, as new crew members always did, tried to sum up his companions. His analysis of his pilot worried him for even on a circuits and bumps pattern he seemed unsure and indecisive. For a time Paddy kept his thoughts to himself. The other four crew members knuckled down to the tasks in hand. As long as the weather held they flew. During all the next eight flights during November Paddy was to act as bomb-aimer. Once again he demonstrated his skill with his quiet, 'Left a little, right a little … steady, steady, bombs gone.' Not only did the crew practise dropping bombs but also air firing which took place off Filey.

December 1942 saw little improvement in the English weather. Further training was thought necessary by those in command. The first flight of the month took place at 11.40 when the Wellington to which they had been allocated lifted into the air. They were to be airborne for three hours while carrying out an oil test and completing air firing off Filey. The next flight was cross-country and after some five hours of night flying the plane was forced to land at Oakley. The pilot was tense but the crew kept silent.

Ferried from Oakley to Harwell took thirty minutes. On the 11th December they were again scheduled to fly Wellington 1093. The crew assembled as usual as the pilot went through the routine checks. Revving the engines, the Wellington trundled forward but didn't get any higher than fifty feet as the flaps had failed to find the right slot. By now the plane was well down the runway and with engines screaming there was little the fraught crew could do. The crash came suddenly as the 'plane thudded into wires and the edge of a forest. Trees were snapped like matchsticks as the aircraft skidded to a halt. All the crew were able to get out and scampered to the nearest stone wall. Just as they flung themselves into its protective shelter the Wellington exploded. Six pairs of eyes watched it burn as they thought of what might have been. Once again Paddy's luck held, but he was now part of a crew which had lost faith in the pilot's ability.

Six days later they were flying again, this time at night, but after their experience of crashing on take-off, they were still concerned about the ability of their pilot. The remaining flights were supposed to be routine night flying exercises. Bomb aiming, gunnery tests and navigational cross-country journeys were part of the nightly routine. Their longest flight was seven hours and five minutes over a blacked-out England.

The weather in January was not suitable for flying and in February Paddy found himself with 428 Squadron at Dalton, Yorkshire. This was a Royal Canadian Air Force Squadron which was part of Six Group of Bomber Command. One of the more remarkable facts about the Royal Canadian Air Force in England was that it was financed entirely by the Canadian Government. This was a tremendous gesture of goodwill towards Great Britain.

Dalton airfield had been closed for six months for redevelopment before the Ghost Squadron of 428 arrived. Each squadron had its own number, badge and motto. The badge of 428 Squadron was symbolised by a skull within a shroud and the words, 'In a shroud, a death's head.' The motto 'Usque ad finem' (to the very end) indicated that this is exactly what the squadron would do. Paddy, after his spell in the Americas, was not unfamiliar with the ways of the Canadians. Happily he settled into his new quarters and awaited events.

Six Group Bomber Command had been formed on January 1st, 1943. On the 4th of February Paddy was scheduled to be the mid-upper gunner on a Wellington mark 111. This was to be piloted by Sergeant Cartier. Their mission was to the town of Lorient, on the south west coast of Brittany. Here the Germans had built a number of U-boat pens which had access to the Atlantic ocean. Well defended and well camouflaged it was not the easiest of targets. Lorient was only one of a number of U-boat bases to be attacked by Bomber Command.

This was Paddy's first mission over enemy territory and one which filled him with trepidation. He had listened to, and observed, those who had flown on missions before. The false humour, the frowns, the rituals and the belief that they were invincible still held. All who flew knew the risks. They knew that one in five would eventually be killed or severely injured. Still, such thoughts had to be hidden and perhaps that accounted for the tense faces. However, the constant training they had undergone would, Paddy believed, ensure that this first flight would be successful. Sergeant Cartier and his crew were briefed by those in command. Such briefings took place some hours before the actual flight. Those crews participating would be addressed by the Intelligence Officer who would give any information known about the target. He would be followed by the Meteorological Officer whose role it was to announce what was known about the weather over Lorient, both on the way there and the way back. Third in line was the Navigational Officer who used a large wall map to point out the route the pilots would take. Following this officer, the Bombing leader spoke and he was followed by the Signals leader, both were pilots who had flown on previous missions. Questions were asked and answered, all accepted their role to give of their best. Finally the crews would be addressed by the Station Commander who would stress the importance of the target and the need for accurate bombing.

It was the weather forecast on such raids that dominated conversation. The weather was perhaps the greatest enemy the bomber had to contend with. So unpredictable was the information given by the Met. Officer that at times it bore little relation to reality. The longer the flight the more the difficulties encountered. Everyone knew what the weather was like on take-off but the forecast for the outward journey would depend on the proposed route and the information from the Met. Office. Flying at anything over ten thousand feet produced problems, of which the greatest was the danger of ice forming on the wings. Pilots tried to keep away from moisture-laden clouds to prevent this happening. Ice on the wings caused the engines and airscrews to be affected. Icing could also result in blocked vision and the rapid lowering of body temperature. Conditions over the target could be vastly different from those given at the briefing. Paddy recalls that it was probably at this stage that there would also be the further challenges of avoiding anti-aircraft defences and enemy fighters. The weather on the return journey, as fuel became a problem, was of great concern for the crew. Fog at base was a major factor in crashes and one could only hope that the Vale of York was free of such a hazard. Time alone would tell.

The crews would pick up their flasks and rations while personal possessions would be handed in at the crew room. The crew of B K 564 would be wearing their flying gear and their hands would be clothed in three layers – silk, wool and then leather. The final item of equipment was their parachute. This was handed to them by a smiling W.A.A.F.

Paddy, along with other members of the crew, was taken to the Wellington bomber by truck. Once on board allocated positions would be taken up. In Paddy's case this was the mid-upper gunners turret. Pre-start checks would then begin. Paddy listened as the pilot went through his routine and realised that this time it was for real.

At briefing they had been told that the U-boat pens at Lorient would be heavily defended and that the weather would be low cloud Not ideal, Paddy thought, as he settled into position. The journey proved something of an anti-climax. Flak was present as they flew over France. It reminded him of his days in the anti-aircraft unit when his searchlight sought out German aircraft. Now he was on the receiving end and it was not enjoyable. The German ground defences had, Paddy was told, been slowly improving their efficiency. Flak presented a number of problems for the air crew primarily because they were unable to retaliate. The pilot of Paddy's Wellington took evasive action by changing the pattern he was flying. Not only were the ground defences improving but attacks by German night fighters became a problem. Paddy, nestled in his gun turret, searched the skies for vapour trails and any sudden attack by Messerschmitts. He also kept an eye open for those on the same mission as themselves, for crashes over enemy territory were not uncommon. Still, they were under orders and one of a number of aircraft approaching the target. At this stage of the war a Pathfinder force had not been formed and it was left to the leading bomber to mark the target. Paddy wondered at the layers of planes, not only above but also below him. Bombing in large numbers presented its own problems. Those in the top layer could, and did, accidentally bomb those below. Not only were 'planes bombed by their own but were frequently set on fire by falling incendiaries. Altogether, missions over enemy territory took some getting used to, and as Sergeant Cartier held the aircraft steady the bombs were released.

Once the bombs had gone the Wellington lurched skywards due to the lightening of its load. Paddy gazed from his turret at the destruction unleashed by his and all the other aircraft involved in the raid. Paddy found that he had been in a cold sweat over the target and he was sure he was not alone. The voices on the intercom during the return journey were subdued but at least they had survived so far. However there was no time for rest as they still maintained a watch for enemy fighters. Many a 'plane had succumbed to post-bombing attacks after releasing the bomb load and relaxing. Tiredness also contributed to fatalities. Once again the German anti-aircraft guns blazed into action at the returning bombers.

Landing at Dalton in the early hours of the morning after such a flight proved straightforward. Recognition signals were transmitted, the under-carriage put into landing mode as the landing lights were switched on. Paddy breathed a sigh of relief as the wheels touched down and the Wellington came to a halt. The sighs of relief were almost audible as the crew left the 'plane. Yet it was still not over. De-briefing, a detailed enquiry into what had happened over the target took place.

Sergeant Cartier gave his report. The rest of the crew chipped in, often with conflicting reports, but on the whole the mission had been successful. Paddy, conscious of the work of others, wandered back to thank the ground crew and then as if bombing enemy territory was an everyday occurrence, tucked into bacon and eggs.

Paddy did not fly for another thirteen days. This interlude gave him an opportunity to explore the airfield at Dalton and sample the hospitality of the nearest town, Thirsk. Situated six miles from the airfield, Thirsk was to prove a magnet for those away from home. The town with its thirteen pubs, ranging from the up-market Golden Fleece Hotel, managed by Mr. and Mrs. Hollington, to that of the small cottage pub that served beer from the front room. The hotels and pubs of the town tended to be divided between officers and other ranks. Monday nights the Golden Fleece Hotel was always full of officers and their wives and girl friends. Mondays were known as steak nights, although where the steaks came from was never divulged. Thirsk had other attractions for the young Irishman. There was the Town Hall where dances to live music were held and cinemas where one could relax and watch Hollywood in action. The town also boasted two market days, Mondays and Saturdays, when stalls would be erected and bargains were to be had, at a price. One of the waitresses at the Golden Fleece recalls that a market stall holder sold black stockings for what seemed like an exorbitant sum. She also remembers that the stockings were always faulty and that one pair she bought had the seams at the side. 'Such is war,' the stall holder said when she complained. Paddy enjoyed the atmosphere of the markets and small shops which before rationing sold a multitude of goods. Thirsk took part in various national fund-raising events such as 'Spitfire Week'. On such occasions the townsfolk would be cajoled into raising enough pounds, shillings and pence to buy a Spitfire. Other similar events included Scrap Metal, Waste Paper and Bottles and Jar weeks. The town suffered one air attack by the Luftwaffe but little damage was done. There was more concern at the number of bombers which had crashed on take-off or landing. His ability to make friends soon brought him a number of invitations to visit families in their own homes.

On Tuesday 19th February,1943 Paddy flew as astro-lookout with Sergeant Manning. This time the target was Wilhemshaven and the crew were to be airborne for six hours and ten minutes. The mission of Wellington B K 156 proved to be the pounding of the docks and U-boat yards. Wilhelmshaven, once the refuge of the German battleship Tirpitz, was a difficult target. On several occasions it had attracted the attention of Bomber Command and Paddy was again in the heat of the action. The weather, German flak and enemy fighters were the main hazards. The relief when they heard, 'bombs gone,' was palpable as the pilot headed back across the North Sea The cold was intense and the resultant pain from such cold very real, as the crew kept a lookout for enemy fighters. Those that still had a flask full of beverage, gladly shared its contents amongst those who had drunk theirs. There was an almost hysterical atmosphere in the 'plane as recognition signals were flashed to the observers on the English coast. Yet it was not to Dalton they were to return. Owing to difficulties at base they were to return to nearby Topcliffe, which was another station that had been developed and updated. Little over a month before it had been handed over to Six Group of the Royal Canadian Air Force. This airfield, a mere two and a half miles from Dalton was to become the controlling station for Dalton, Topcliffe and Dishforth aerodromes.

Landing on an unfamiliar airfield early in the morning presents problems. Many bombers, due to lack of fuel or being shot-up over enemy territory, together with fatigue, crashed on return. Many a crew gave thanks to the designers of the bombers for their robustness and their ability to get home with a skilful pilot when all seemed lost, but Sergeant Manning landed the bomber without mishap as the crew stretched their cramped limbs. Inside the 'plane there was silence for a while, then slowly each member of the crew made his way to the door and clambered out. The ground crew were waiting as was the transport to take them for their de-briefing. The chatter resumed as the crew reported on their mission over enemy territory. Finally it was time for bacon and eggs and then sleep. Paddy sighed as he fell into bed thankful that his second mission had been successful, although for the Group it was not without loss.

On 20th February Paddy was ordered to report to the R.A.F. station at Driffield to attend an Air Bombers course. Driffield, an old established airfield was due to have new runways constructed. However with 1484 Flight, Paddy had to undertake daily training on map reading, dual flying and the dropping of bombs. The weather at this time was pretty awful and only eleven hours of airborne activity could be achieved. At the end of this training Paddy's skills were assessed as average.

Returning to Dalton, Paddy was told he would be acting as astro-lookout under Sergeant Manning for a raid on St. Nazaire. This coastal town, some miles south of Lorient and six miles up the Loire estuary, was yet another U-boat base for the Germans. Although it had fewer facilities than Lorient, the base at St. Nazaire was heavily defended. Not only were the U-boats safely tucked into their concrete pens, but the whole area was viciously defended by anti-aircraft batteries and many, many searchlights. Thus, on the last day of February, Paddy was a crew member of a Wellington bomber equipped with mines. They were on a 'gardening' mission. This meant the laying of mines near the coast to prevent the breakout of enemy submarines. The operation would mean that the attacking bombers would be in layers ranging from10,000 feet to over 20,000 feet. The dangers of such layers were inherent, not only on the flight but also over the target. A number would collide, others due to technical problems would turn back, while still others would present ideal targets for German fighters.

From his position in the upper turret Paddy gazed at a sky filled with flying machines. His role was to warn of any approaching enemy and he also had the responsibility of operating a machine gun. Opposition fighters together with the anti-aircraft defences, would try to break up the formation. As the enemy fighters flitted in and out of the layers of planes an air gunner was fortunate if he could get an accurate burst fired. Paddy remembers the red-tiled roofs of the houses as they were hit with incendiaries and the damage that had been done to the factories and roads. Later reports indicated that the U-boat pens had not been damaged.

Almost seven hours after take-off Sergeant Manning landed the 'plane at Topcliffe. Once again the ritual of de-briefing followed, then that most welcome of meals, bacon and eggs, hot tea and toast. The 28th February had proved to be a busy day.

Chapter Eight

The Vale of York was, during the Second World war, littered with airfields. Each had its role to play in the battle against Germany and the occupied countries. Large tracts of land had been commandeered to create the airfields. Farms and houses were demolished, trees and hedges uprooted and roads diverted as new power supplies were laid. The runways, some thousands of yards in length, dominated each airfield. Initially of grass but quickly converted to concrete as the planes grew in size and weight, the runways were laid according to the direction of the prevailing winds and were accessed via taxi-ways.

Each airfield, housing perhaps two and a half thousand personnel, was a self-contained unit with its own generators, sewage system and underground fuel tanks. A number of airfields had been built at great speed while the few which had been established prior to 1939 were extended. There was the usual control tower, while nearby would be the fire and ambulance section. The latter would be on full alert during take-off and landing, at which times crashes were frequent and often fatal.

Accommodation blocks were either of brick or Nissen-type construction. The latter were heated by the traditional pot-bellied stove fed with coal or coke which was always in short supply. Nearby the cook-house and mess halls were built ready to operate at all hours. Certain huts would act as a place of worship, a cinema or a theatre. The air force did not neglect the health of those who served as there was also a gymnasium and a station sick-quarters.

Other buildings were allocated to the armoury, the motor transport section, the engineers, safety, clothing and parachutes. The WAAF's accepted responsibility for the packing of these and the 'chutes were inspected and hung out at set intervals At one airfield in Yorkshire there had been an incident in the parachute hut. One of the WAAFs, a German sympathiser, had been discovered deliberately packing the parachutes incorrectly, which made them unworkable. The WAAF in question was taken away by the Military Police and no more was heard of her. The WAAFs had their separate accommodation and shower blocks. The aircraft were provided with specially hardened shelters and away from the buildings was the bomb dump, usually protected by grass banks and thick brick walls. The Station Commander had full responsibility for all that happened within the perimeter fence.

Paddy Johnston had experienced life on a number of stations, not only in Yorkshire but throughout the country and it was with such an airfield that Paddy became all too familiar. Some of his leisure time was spent on the airfields. Here facilities existed for indoor and outdoor activities and Paddy enjoyed many a game of cards or billiards. Other organisations were also involved in providing recreation for aircrew and ground staff. The N.A.A.F.I., the Salvation Army and E.N.S.A. were but some of the organisations involved. E.N.S.A. (Entertainments National Service Association) used to stage plays, song and dance displays, variety shows and readings. Paddy remembers some excellent performances at such events. Such entertainment lifted the morale of those they served. The camp cinema would revive memories of Paddy's visits to the pictures in Belfast although now he did not have to pay in jam jars. Films such as 'In Which We Serve' or 'In Society' with Abbot and Costello would take his mind off events in the sky. The Y.M.C.A. would offer alternate films to those shown on the station cinema screen. Occasionally one of the hangars would, for a time, be converted into a roller-skating rink. There would be much hilarity as those inexperienced in the art of roller skating ended up in a crumpled heap. Dances would also be held. For such occasions buses would be laid on to enable girls in neighbouring towns and villages to add their presence to those of the WAAFs. A number of these dances would be with live bands, such as Glenn Miller, while others used gramophone records. Paddy would demonstrate his dancing skills at either event. A weekly bulletin advertising all functions was displayed on various notice boards.

Every few weeks, if they survived, those who flew the planes were granted leave. Should this be a seven day pass, then Paddy returned to Belfast. Once there he would stay with one of his cousins and regale his relations with tales of his adventures. On shorter passes a weekend might be spent in London with his friends. On such visits he would see the damage the German Luftwaffe was continuing to cause with its bomb attacks. However, he was heartened by the spirit demonstrated by the people of the capital as they continued about their everyday tasks.

One of the problems of life in the air force was that crews were moved from station to station as the need arose. Planes would be damaged, others fail to return either as a result of enemy action, lack of fuel or the death of a crew member. Little was said as the names of those who failed to return were wiped off the board and their belongings packed away to be sent back to their families.

The raids over enemy territory increased in number. Each station would provide a number of aircraft and crew until the required number of planes were assembled. The roar of the engines would waken those who tried to sleep as the bombers took off on another mission. The losses in aircrew by Bomber Command during the war were high – fifty five thousand killed and nine thousand wounded. Those that flew knew the risk but as Paddy said, 'We had a job to do and we got on with it.'

Many families in Yorkshire played host to servicemen. When not working, crews would wander the villages and chat to the locals. Young boys would be awe-struck at the sight of aircrew and small talk would be exchanged as requests for candy or even a pair of wings insignia would be made. Paddy remembers lying on the grass with other crew members waiting to board the Lancaster, and watching the village youths scramble through the barbed wire perimeter fence. The usual topic of conversation, once the youngsters had persuaded the crew not to give them away to the guards, was to ask the local boys whether they had any sisters. The answer was always 'Yes – and we'll introduce you when we get back if you will take us on this trip.' On one occasion the R.A.F. police managed to 'arrest' a group of village boys and haul them off to the guard room, where they were severely admonished. In the village of Topcliffe the Y.M.C.A. operated a canteen above the old toll booth. Those on active service could pop in for sandwiches, drinks and company. One of the young lady helpers, who rather fancied herself and seemed overawed by so many eligible young men, tended to respond to requests for sandwiches in an affected accent. She once replied to such a request with 'Hem, Jem, or Spem' (ham, jam or Spam) but fortunately those who asked accepted her response as normal. A record was set one night when one of the helpers, Margaret Burton, poached sixty eggs and toasted sixty slices of bread using only a small battered pan and a single toaster. The lady volunteers who manned the canteen were astounded when the Canadians asked for a mixture of coffee, tea and hot chocolate to drink. It was also the first time the locals had heard of peanut butter.

Certainly village life was transformed by the arrival of the Royal Canadian Air Force. The sight and sound of the planes was a constant reminder of their presence. Many a village bicycle was stolen for a quick ride back to the airfield after a night out at the local pub. The cycles were generally recovered from beneath a hedgerow near the camp. Villagers became accustomed to seeing trolley-loads of bombs being trundled through the village on their way to the airfields.

Many of the mothers in the towns and villages who had sons and daughters of their own serving in the forces would offer to wash and mend the clothes of those that flew the planes. Relationships were established and a number of married servicemen, once they had permission, brought their wives to Yorkshire hoping to find a billet in a local home.

The City of York was one of the venues to which members of 6 Bomber Group found their way. A favourite haunt of Paddy and his friends was Betty's Tea Rooms, still in existence and still serving excellent tea and cakes. The legacy of some aircrew may be found by examining the names scratched on a large mirror. Nearer to some airfields was the market town of Thirsk with its pubs, cinemas, dances and socials. Such venues provided welcome relaxation for both service personnel and the civilian population The dance bands would play tunes such as 'Moonlight Becomes You', 'If I Had My Way' or 'Give a Little Whistle' from the film 'Pinocchio.' Voices would be raised in song and feet would be tapping. Many a romance began in Thirsk Town Hall when live bands played while civilians and service personnel danced to the latest music. One romance was that of Joan Bradley and Paddy Johnston. Perhaps it

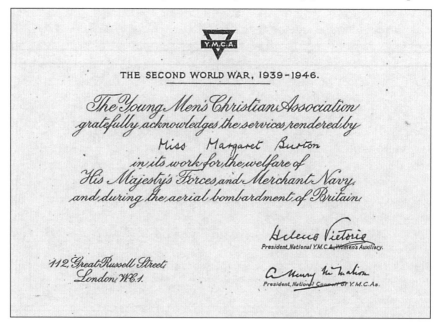

was during a quickstep or a foxtrot that the relationship began. Neither can recall any particular tune that was to mark the start of their love affair. That spring in 1943 there was a certain chemistry between the Sergeant in blue and Joan in her dress. There was no lack of conversation as the two spun round the dance floor. Paddy discovered that Joan was the youngest of five children and was a local girl. Her mother ran the Mowbray Café which was also a bakers and confectioners shop in Kirkgate. The café was well-known to the army and air force servicemen and women. A number of officers were billeted opposite, who, when the opportunity arose, would go out shooting and bring their trophies for Mrs. Bradley to cook. Rabbit, hare and pheasant were made into pies and casseroles, much to the delight of the shooters.

Joan's father worked for the Electricity Board and was no mean cricketer. However Paddy really wanted to know about the girl in his arms and a further meeting was arranged. He was full of trepidation on the journey back to camp, for he knew that he would be called upon to fly again. Joan also knew of the dangers of going out with any member of a bomber crew. She had seen enough airmen go missing – many forever.

Working as a clerk at the District Command of Royal Engineers, Joan Bradley was an attractive, petite lady. She was due to celebrate her twenty-first birthday in May and rather than be conscripted, had already applied to join the Wrens. The smart, dark blue naval uniform with black stockings and cap worn at a jaunty angle, together with the possibility of travel, appealed to the young Miss Bradley. On their next meeting Paddy listened to tales of her schooling, her performances in the local church socials, her work in the shop and her ambitions for the future. He, in turn, delighted her with tales of Ireland and of his time in the R.A.F. and the army. Further meetings were arranged and both realised that they were in love. This was not a wise thing to do for war can be cruel to lovers. Courtship was not made easy in 1943. Paddy had his flying duties while Joan not only worked in the office but also helped her mother in the cafe. She also worked as a volunteer for the Y.M.C.A. in Castle Garth. This building was also a venue for dances. Dancing was one of the prime leisure pursuits of the young. Paddy and Joan would board a train at Thirsk and travel to either Knaresborough or Harrogate in order to dance to tunes and songs performed by national and regional bands. One of the problems on returning to Thirsk was that the black-out was strictly enforced. Frequently Paddy or Joan or both would bump into lamp posts and apologise. Nevertheless time was found when the young lovers could be together. Walks in the countryside, listening to the antics of Rob Wilton as Mr. Muddlecome on the wireless, and watching Eric Portman in 'The 49th Parallel' were some of the pleasures they enjoyed. Paddy and Joan continued to dance and the fox-trot and the quickstep became their favourites. When the time came to dance to 'Who's Taking You Home Tonight' both knew the answer. Joan and Paddy decided to become engaged in May, 1943. Before that could happen, certain formalities had to be followed. Paddy had to ask Mr. Jack Bradley for his youngest daughter's hand. He gave his approval and great were the celebrations in the mess and the Bradley household. However, their plans suffered a setback when Joan was conscripted into the Wrens and ordered to report to Blundellsands. Letters were written, promises made, attempts to meet, sometimes successful, were made while the couple planned for their future.

Chapter Nine

In June 1943 Sergeant Paddy Johnston was ordered to attend Number 22 O.T.U. (Operational Training Unit), at Gaydon in the Midlands. Here he was to chum up with Sergeant Jack Mill, a pilot in the R.C.A.F. Jack was short of a crew member and Paddy asked if he could be taken aboard. He was and a bond was formed which would last the lifetime of both men.

Paddy was to be rear gunner and bomb-aimer to pilot Jack Mill who flew Wellington bombers. Throughout June eight training exercises were undertaken. These ranged from daylight hours when low level bombing was practised to over nine hours of night flying when high level bombing was the order of the day.

In July Paddy and Jack were posted to the Royal Canadian Air Force station at Croft, for a conversion course to the Halifax bomber. This was a four-engined bomber with a crew of seven – pilot, navigator, air bomber, flight engineer, wireless operator, mid-upper gunner and rear gunner. Planes continued to grow in size as did the bomb load they could carry. The changes in aircraft meant that the crews were continually up-dating their knowledge and skills. Each plane, as was common with all bombers, would be designated a letter, for example C for Charlie, F for Freddie or T for Tommy. These were an aid to identification. Recording the time of take-off of the planes was vital and to ensure accuracy a runway caravan would be positioned at the end of the runway. Not only did those inside the caravan respond to problems but also acted as checkers when the aircraft returned. Probably the most common problem encountered was the failure of the undercarriage to descend,. which could be due to pilot error or enemy damage. Should this happen a red Verey flare would be fired which indicated to the pilot that he should go round again to try to release the undercarriage. If this was not possible then the crew and those on the station prepared for a crash landing.

During his time at Croft Paddy acted as bomb aimer and second pilot. About twenty-six hours of daylight flying took place but just over eight hours of night flying. Practice in cross-country navigation, local bombing, air firing. and fighter affiliation also continued. On his bomb-aiming tests Paddy secured a satisfactory 75%.

August saw Paddy posted to 408 Squadron at Leeming, another R.C.A.F. squadron. The badge of 408 Squadron was a Canada goose volant, while the motto read – 'For Freedom'. Paddy remembered from his time in Canada that the Canada goose was a powerful flyer that covered vast distances during migration. Paddy was once again flying with Jack on Halifaxes with the crew, practising and honing their skills. In September Jack Mill was promoted from Sergeant to Warrant Officer and the bond between the two men strengthened. It was also the month when they were introduced to G.E.E. This navigational aid would, if used correctly, assist in the accuracy of positioning the aircraft in the air. Not only was Paddy continuing his training but he was now one of those servicemen waiting anxiously for mail from 'his girl'. He was not disappointed. He was also welcomed into the Bradley home whenever he was in Thirsk.

This bustling town became his second home. Here he and Joan would wander round the market place gazing at the goods on display. They were familiar with B. Smiths, one of the oldest department stores in the country. A huge thirty-thousand-gallon water tank, erected as an additional source of water for the Fire Brigade in case of air raids, was a familiar sight in the Market Place On many an occasion it would be used as a rubbish dump and on one memorable occasion Paddy remembers, a special police constable was given a ducking by some high-spirited Canadians. Paddy and Joan would meet whenever their military masters decided that they were entitled to leave. It was not an easy time for the young couple, but it was an exciting time for the Irishman. He now had utter confidence in his pilot, was a member of a good crew, had a number of operational tours in his log book and was in love.

In September Warrant Officer Mill introduced his crew to the Lancaster. Still with 408 Squadron, it was a plane which crew members would remember with affection. Paddy spent some twenty one hours familiarising himself with this four-engined bomber. Powered by four Rolls Royce Merlin engines, the Lancaster was to prove an asset to those who were entrusted with its potential. This was a plane which could deliver some 18,000 pounds of high explosives and from its four fuel tanks feed over 2,000 gallons to the engines. Although introduced in 1942, this was the crew's first experience of handling such an aircraft.

Seven crew members were needed to fly V for Victor, to which they had been assigned. Jack Mill took his seat as pilot almost twenty feet from the ground, gazed around the cockpit and wondered why no-one had thought of it before. Alongside him and acting as second pilot was the Flight Engineer. Further back in a curtained-off area sat the navigator with his charts and instruments. Protecting the plane were the gunners in their perspex blisters, one at the rear of the plane and one placed in the mid-upper position. Paddy, as bomb aimer, lay under the fuselage in the nose of the aircraft looking for signs to help the navigator and ready to use not only the-aiming sights, but also the Browning machine guns. The space between the navigator and the rear gunner would, over time, be filled with electric gadgetry.

September 4th, 1943 was Paddy's first flight in a Lancaster. He watched as the trolley accumulator was plugged in and the 1640 horsepower engines were fired in sequence. Then Jack began the pre-flight checks, among which were pressures and temperatures, directional finder compass, oxygen regulator, bomb doors plus many others vital to their safety. The plane taxied to its take-off position and waited for the green light. Paddy found that the Lancaster was indeed an aircraft to be proud of. During its first year of operations it was beginning to develop a sort of folk lore with its ability to survive – this in spite of poor escape hatches and high loss rate. As training continued, Paddy, when high altitude flying was scheduled, would dress with as many layers of clothes as possible. In spite of such layers the cold was intense and the fear of the machine guns and other mechanisms icing-up was very real. Frostbite was a threat that Paddy had little to combat.

Joan Bradley, now a Wren, had been busy. A wedding ceremony had been arranged, postponed because of duties and re-arranged, subject to both being able to get leave. The ceremony was to be at St. Mary's Church in Thirsk. The date the young couple had agreed on was the seventh of October, followed by a honeymoon in London. Preparations in the Bradley household went ahead.

Michaelmas Day 1943 saw Paddy flying in Q for Queenie as front gunner. The purpose of this training flight was to gain further experience with G.E.E. After two hours all seemed satisfactory and his thoughts turned to the wedding. Joan and he had been granted leave and Paddy had booked a room at the Russell Hotel, London, for their honeymoon. Not only that but he was now a Flight Sergeant.

At eleven o'clock on Thursday, the seventh of October, 1943 Paddy and Joan were married by Canon Broughton 'for better for worse, for richer for poorer, till death us do part.' Joan, in a dress made by a local couturier, presented a picture of radiance. It was a ceremony Paddy will never forget as, dressed in his blue R.A.F. uniform with his hard-earned Observers half wing above his left breast, he did his Squadron proud, apart from one item. In his haste to get to the Church on time he had neglected to change into his shoes and was married in his service boots.

The newly weds in Trafalgar Square

Paddy

Survival!

Joan

The Wedding

Joan forgave him. Paddy's companions in the air did not make the ceremony. They had celebrated the forthcoming marriage of their bomb aimer too well in York the night before and had missed the train to Thirsk. Paddy had wisely declined an invitation to join them and instead stayed with one of Joan's cousins. The wedding reception was held at the Bradley home and in spite of restrictions with rationing, it became a grand wartime celebration. After changing into her travelling outfit and a round of frantic good-byes, Joan and her new husband caught a train from Thirsk station to London.

The starry-eyed couple booked into their hotel and began a hectic sight-seeing tour of the capital. They fed the pigeons in Trafalgar Square, visited Kew Gardens and went to the theatre and cinema. 'Random Harvest' and 'For Whom The Bell Tolls' had been released and were attracting filmgoers, while at the theatre, Terence Rattigan's 'While The Sun Shines' continued to pull in audiences. It was the time of the music of Glenn Miller and the honeymooners danced to the music of some of the London bands and such hits as 'You were Never Lovelier', and 'Moonlight Becomes You' and the ever popular 'In The Mood'.

Paddy, still questing for knowledge, decided to take his bride to the Science Museum. Joan remembers the visit as the most boring time of the whole week. As Paddy and Joan explored the capital, the damage caused by the German bombers was plain to see. St. Paul's Cathedral had miraculously survived the blitz and the spirit of the Londoners never wavered. Such spirit gave the newly-married couple hope for the future. The seven days passed all too quickly. Joan had to report back to Londonderry while for Paddy it was back to Bomber Command.

Eleven days after their marriage Paddy was once again, bomb aimer for Jack Mill. Paddy had a suspicion that T for Tommy was due for a long flight as the reported fuel intake was over 2,000 gallons. The mission that night was Hanover. The station Commander had, at the briefing, emphasised the importance of the target. In Hanover were centred large machine works and tyre manufactories. On the 18th October T for Tommy, fully laden, took to the air. Whatever else Paddy remembers about the position of the bomb aimer in a Lancaster his main memory was the bitter cold. Sidcot flying suits over as many clothes as possible resulted in a grotesque appearance. However, the bomb-aimers panel, with its rows of selector switches and timing device, was there to be operated by his trained hands. The bombs, whether heavy 4,000 pounders or the much smaller incendiaries, were housed in the thirty-three feet long bomb bay. It was vital to all concerned that the bombs were released in the right order. This would ensure the stability of the plane Once the bombs had gone and photographic evidence had been obtained, then it was back to base, but unfortunately not to Joan.

Two days later Paddy was on another mission over Germany. This time the target was Leipzig, an important industrial town producing ball-bearings and housing Messerschmitt factories. T for Tommy was again fuelled up and prepared for its seven-hour flight. With a plane taking off every two minutes ready to assemble in the sky for yet another massive bombing raid on Germany's industrial heartland, Paddy reflected on the pep talk they had listened to at the briefing. The Station Commander stressed that the war still had a long way to go and reminded them that they were fighting for the freedom of the democratic world. Paddy agreed as he checked on another task he had to perform. This was the dropping, through a special chute, of an anti-radar device known as 'window'. This was strips of thin black paper coated on one side with aluminium which when dropped in thousands of pieces caused a 'blip' on German airborne and ground screens and which caused confusion among the enemy's defence.

Communication within the bomber was by intercom. Occasionally there would be idle chatter but generally one had to be alert to avoid mid-air collisions, be aware that enemy fighters may be prowling and be on guard in case of flak damage. All in all a mission of over 1,000 miles would produce intense bursts of activity amidst long hours of listening to the roar of the plane's engines. Paddy witnessed planes being shot out of the sky while others took evasive action after being coned by searchlights. His words 'bombs gone' acted like a tonic to the crew as Jack Mill added, 'Let's get the hell out of here.'

Paddy's last mission that October of 1943 was to Kassel, an industrial centre for assembling fighter planes. It was also an important railway centre. Instead of flying in T for Tommy they were ordered to fly W for Whisky. As in all aircrew there were superstitions. Some would only climb into the plane on their right foot while others would carry lucky charms. In spite of the change of plane the crew had confidence in one another and believed that they would survive. Yet again the bowsers pumped thousands of gallons of fuel into the tanks. The ground crew had been swarming over W for Whisky since the early hours. The station, aware that there was another raid on Germany, became alive with anticipation. Armourers 'bombed up' the Lancaster with the necessary load while others checked the engines, the bomb doors, the guns and other areas essential to the smooth flight of the aircraft. Those involved in the preparations were aware of the importance of what they did and had great respect for the crew that flew the plane.

Kassel, like other German industrial towns, was heavily defended. A centre known for its ability to assemble fighters, it also had essential rail links to other industrial areas. The crew of W for Whisky were uncertain of her. There was no logical reason for this but crews became familiar with the idiosyncrasies of a particular plane. However, as usual, those on board got on with the task in hand. Paddy remembers Kassel, as it was visible miles before they reached it. With the bombs and incendiaries dropped by those ahead, a firestorm had been created on the ground. After the words, 'bombs away,' Jack Mill swung for home. This was always a traumatic time. Enemy fighters would be lurking ready to harry and shoot down the unwary. Even those who were fully alert were often caught unawares as bullets peppered the aircraft – sometimes with fatal results. Not only was there a danger from the enemy but also the prospect of running out of fuel. Jack Mill, pilot of W for Whisky, knew how to conserve fuel. Just how he did this no-one quite knew. As the coast of England loomed below, lack of fuel was definitely a problem. Nursing the Lancaster with skill, Jack decided that returning to base would be risky. The plane was diverted to Rufforth airfield. Rufforth was a satellite airfield of Marston Moor just west of York. The Lancaster had almost made it home. Paddy found it was a welcome relief to listen to the silence as the engines shut down. He wondered if there would be a letter from Joan that day.

T for Tommy was back in action three days after the raid on Kassel for a flight test lasting just over one and a half hours. The first operational flight in November, 1943 took place two days before Guy Fawkes night. The powers-that-be had decided that a large force would target Dusseldorf. Dusseldorf was a prime industrial area, situated on the Rhine, which boasted a large inland port. Paddy watched as the early morning rituals began. Weather conditions in the Vale of York were not good. Low lying mist and fog frequently meant the cancellation of a mission. This caused frustration to the ground crew, who had spent many hours preparing the plane, often in dreadful conditions. To the aircrew a cancellation caused anger and despair combined with a sense of relief. On this occasion all went smoothly as the planes were loaded with their deadly bombs and the aircrew were briefed about the problems they were likely to encounter on their flight over enemy territory. Just before dusk T for Tommy was given clearance for take-off and Jack Mill eased the Lancaster into the air.

Dusseldorf, some four hundred miles from base meant, that if all went well, an outward flight of over two hours. As the planes rose above twelve thousand feet, the oxygen masks would be switched on and the cold became more intense. Lack of oxygen resulted in a slow reaction to events and the life of the crew would be in jeopardy. As the protective screen around the target began to respond to yet another bombing raid, the navigator would inform the pilot and the bomb-aimer that they had ten minutes to target. Paddy directed the pilot until he was certain of hitting the target. On this occasion the bombs failed to drop and he remembers cursing as he stamped on the mechanism. He watched with relief as the bombs finally left their bays and he crawled back to his position. It had been an uncomfortable few minutes and for a moment he had thought that Joan might become a widow. His luck held as the plane flew home.

On 18th, November, 408 Squadron was to provide part of an attacking force on the capital of Germany, Berlin. Such a raid involved, for those who survived, a journey of over twelve hundred miles. That it was a vital target no-one doubted. Factories abounded, with names like Siemens, Dornier, Daimler-Benz, and Zeiss held in high regard. However well regarded, these factories produced ammunition, radios, artillery and tanks as well as a host of other military equipment. Berlin, covering almost 900 square miles, had a large urban population. Because of its high profile as an industrial and communication centre it was believed by Bomber Command that its destruction would break the morale of the German people.

Paddy knew, as did the other crew members, that Berlin was a very heavily defended city. Talk among the crews was of heavy flak, numerous searchlights and attacking Messerschmitt 110 and Focke – Wulf 190 night fighters. Not only that, but the Germans were adept at disguising targets by constructing decoys in various places. Still, the raid had been planned. Four hundred Lancasters, the aircrew were told, were to participate in the raid together with a number of Mosquitoes. Such a force, when assembled, would stretch over many miles as each plane kept to its allotted position. On the one thousand bomber raids the attacking force might be fifty miles in length, some two and a half miles in depth and perhaps five miles wide, presenting an awesome sight as it flew over enemy territory. The clowning in the mess the night before seemed a distant memory as the crew of T for Tommy settled down to the serious business of flying. Berlin was to be attacked that night but also Ludwigshafen and Mannheim, as it was believed that this would provide a diversionary tactic to the Berlin raid. Some planes never reached their target. Overheated engines, oxygen failure, frozen guns and icing-up were all causes for planes to return to base. Occasionally a pilot or member of his crew would be accused of 'lack of moral fibre' (L.M.F.), and would be whisked away from the station. Certainly the hours inside the Lancaster seemed like an eternity. Over the target nerves would be stretched to breaking point.

T for Tommy gave no cause for concern during the pre-flight checks. Dusk fell over the Vale of York and the sound of revving engines disturbed the birds which had already gone to roost. Always there was someone to wave you off in the gathering gloom. The crew were not disappointed as arms were raised to salute those on their way to Berlin.

Climbing steadily T for Tommy reached 22,000 feet and levelled off. A number of Lancasters had been equipped with the new H 2S equipment which would help in greater precision bombing. Paddy and his flying companions kept up a constant chatter until Jack's voice came over the intercom telling them to concentrate.

The Germans had taken to dropping parachute flares which left the Lancasters clear targets for enemy fighters and ack-ack. Low cloud hindered the attack despite the marking of Berlin by the Mosquitoes. The raid was not helped by the failure of the H 2S equipment. Once again 408 did its best and losses were low. Paddy took part in two further raids on Berlin on the 22nd and 23rd of November. On each occasion emotions ran high as the crew endured flak, near misses and attacks by fighters. Thanks to Jack's skill as a pilot, T for Tommy returned each time to base.

Paddy reflected, as December arrived, that he had journeyed a long way from his days on the Shankill Road. His luck still held for had he not married the most beautiful girl in Yorkshire? He did not dwell too much on the future as he had seen too many aircrew blown out of the sky. Just how quickly bed spaces and personal belongings were cleared still amazed him. Still, he had some leave due.

Now at Linton-on-Ouse and still with 408 Squadron (Goose), Paddy was the bomb aimer for Jack Mill in their favourite bomber, T for Tommy. The target that early December was Berlin. This was Paddy's fourth trip over the German capital and his sixteenth over enemy territory. At briefing they were told that they were to be part of a large force of 458 aircraft plus 18 Mosquitoes and their orders were to take advantage of a non-moon night while dropping their bombs. The take-off, scheduled for late afternoon, did not augur well. Fog was drifting over the Vale of York and a number of planes were unable to take to the air.

As the heavily laden bombers flew over the North Sea, clouds began to form which persisted the higher they flew. This resulted in icing on a number of planes, causing them to return home. T for Tommy pressed on as Jack tried to compensate for the strong wind. He also warned those in their perspex blisters to be on the look-out for enemy fighters. At this time the Luftwaffe had been improving their night flying skills which meant that a greater number of Allied planes were being shot down. By plotting the direction of the planes the enemy was able to work out whether the target was Berlin or some other industrial centre. They then alerted the night fighters which patrolled the sky assisted by the probing searchlights. Once coned, flak and tracers would pound the planes and the fighters would go in for the kill. Much depended on the skill of the pilot and the alertness of the crew at these times. The noise of tracer bullets, exploding aircraft and flak competed with the throb of the bomber's engines. As Paddy remarked, 'It was a frightening and confusing time.'

The return flight was almost as bad. Enemy fighters tracked the Lancasters across occupied territory, attacking at every opportunity. Tracers like twinkling lights zipping through the air would bring to the unwary their own death and destruction. Balloon cables were another hazard, for Paddy had seen many a wing from a bomber float past and he would thank his lucky stars that it wasn't from T for Tommy. Paddy knew when he released the bombs from 20,000 feet that he was not sure he had hit the right target. Only the photograph and the debriefing would prove otherwise. It was an awful night for the recently married Paddy. His mind raced back to his time with the British Expeditionary Force when he had been sent to France to make up numbers. Perhaps he was right, for losses on this raid were almost 9%, some forty aircraft. Jack Mill nursed their plane to a safe landing at another airfield. It was not until the 4th of December that the crew found themselves back at base, thankful to be alive.

In spite of the rotten weather the crew flew three training missions during December. Linton-on-Ouse airfield, now under the command of Group Captain W. A. Jones of the R.C.A.F., had been open for six years. Although it had a large number of permanent buildings it also had its share of Nissen huts. Some of the accommodation was occupied by members of the R.C.A.F. – Womens Division. These well-trained volunteers did a tremendous job of work carrying out similar duties to those of the WAAF. The WAAFs had also great faith in the future as they tended the allotments they had created.

On the 20th of December T for Tommy took to the air once more on an operational flight to Frankfurt. Six days before Paddy had celebrated his twenty-fourth birthday and wondered if he would live to see his twenty-fifth. He was aware that the losses in Bomber Command were high. The letters N.Y.R., (not yet returned) on the briefing board would quite often be rubbed out and replaced with 'missing'. However there was a spirit abroad of 'press on regardless,' and he was determined, together with the rest of the crew, to give of his best. The crew listened intently at the briefing session as Christmas was only five days away and they did not want to miss any of the planned entertainment. The weather forecast during this period was not good – cloud, rain, snow and ice, conditions which did not favour accurate bombing. Paddy remembers little of this raid. His log book shows that he was in the air for five hours thirty-five minutes. The reports at debriefing indicated that substantial damage had occurred, not only to the targets but also to houses, rendering thousands of workers homeless.

After this mission Paddy was promoted to Pilot Officer and granted a welcome spell of leave. He was given a warrant to travel to Londonderry and sent a telegram to Joan to say he was on his way. Joan, now in her smart Wren's uniform, was thrilled and she applied for a sleeping-out pass. This was refused by her 'bitch' of an officer. When Paddy arrived at the camp Joan told him what had happened so they decided to attend a dance on the camp. While dancing with her officer husband, Joan's officer appeared. Taking one look at Joan's partner, 'the bitch' changed her mind. As Paddy then remarked, 'It was a case of up with the lark and to bed with a wren.' It was also their first Christmas together.

By the end of the month Paddy had returned to active service at Linton-on-Ouse, flying with Pilot Officer Jack Mill.

Chapter Ten

If Air Chief Marshal Sir Arthur Harris, in charge of Bomber Command, was to be believed, then following the continuing blitz on Berlin, the war would soon be over. Taking part in that blitz were Jack Mill and Paddy Johnston, both now Pilot Officers.

On New Years day, 1944, both flew over Berlin, releasing further destruction on to an already battered city. They were part of a force of four hundred and twenty Lancasters and those who reached the target spent only fourteen minutes there. It seemed a short time in a journey which had lasted over seven hours. The weather, no matter what had been said at base, was unpredictable. The ordered route over Holland did not please those who flew the Lancasters. A tail wind did little to lessen the threat of attacks by German fighters. So it proved, as the crew of E.Q.T. witnessed attacks on themselves and other planes, often with fatal results. The crew were tired, irritable and tense but under orders to bomb Berlin. The take-off from base had been delayed and this had added to the stress.

Harried by German fighters all the way to the target, Paddy remembers the flak, the searchlights and the tracers in the night sky. These provided illumination of sorts but the Lancasters that had been attacked and hit added their own exploding carcasses to the scene. It was a grim time but they bombed the target the Pathfinders had lit. It was an unsatisfactory raid and Paddy blessed his luck as Jack landed at Linton-on-Ouse.

There was little rest either for the aircrew or those who worked on the maintenance and servicing of the planes. Twenty three hours and nineteen minutes after landing, Paddy was airborne once more. The target – Berlin. The unpredictable weather continued as snow covered the Vale of York. It all looked so clean and unsoiled but there was some disbelief that the capital of Germany was again the target. Tiredness can kill, even the prescribed Benzedrine tablets had difficulty in convincing those who took them that their alertness was improved. Due to a communication mix up some sixty bombers, after jettisoning their bombs, returned to base. Two Lancasters crashed on take-off, killing all fourteen young crew members. This was hardly surprising when a plane, fully laden with fuel, bombs and ammunition, exploded.

The ordered route was over the North Sea and Holland and then to Berlin, a journey of six hundred and fifty miles for our recently married Irishman. The weather was foul, cloud coupled with freezing icy conditions made flying difficult. Difficult was an understatement, for German night fighters attacked the force in large numbers over the target. The sound of the flak and the sight of the tracer bullets through the night air sent a shiver of fear through those who flew thousands of feet above an almost unseen Berlin. Unseen, not because of the Pathfinders, but because of the flares dropped by the enemy. This left the bombers exposed, for in spite of their courage, retaliation and evasive action, twenty six bombers were lost. It was a harrowing mission.

Nervous, tense and twitchy, Paddy joined the crew with Jack on the sixth of January,1944. Orders from above were initially for Berlin but later in the day that order was changed and Stettin became the named target. This was the third flight over Germany in six days. Early January with its intense cold, low cloud and uncertain forecasts did little to bolster the confidence of those who flew the Lancasters. Harris, as their chief, was determined to justify his policy of continuing heavy raids on well-defended targets in spite of the recent heavy losses.

By now Paddy was so accustomed to the ritual of the briefing that he was almost blase. This was his first mission to Stettin and would, if the weather forecast was correct, entail a flight of about eight hours. Once again personal possessions were handed in and parachutes collected from the ever-smiling WAAFs. Due to the rapidity of the raids a number of Lancasters had proved not air-worthy, in spite of the strenuous efforts of the ground crew. The gharrys dropped off the crew just after 23.00 hours and Paddy smiled as they waddled towards their aircraft. A full load of fuel coupled with a full load of bombs made for a difficult take-off. The orders had been to fly direct and again those on board had no idea of the advance in German technology. So successful had been the dropping of "Window" in confusing the enemy that the German scientists had been searching for a counter-measure, they had now found a solution – an airborne radar set. This was known as S.N.-2 and a large number of German night fighters were equipped with it. From now on the Germans would carry out a policy which was named – 'Tame Boar'.

Equipped with S.N.-2 the twin-engined German night fighters were able to track the Lancasters along their proposed route. This was co-ordinated with the ground radar and the targets identified. Thus, the fighters, especially the longer-ranged Junkers 88's, together with the use of dim tracers, meant that those protecting German industrial areas had distinct advantages unknown to those who flew the bombers. Reports of bombers spiralling out of control for no apparent reason became more common. Paddy remembers heavy flak, probing searchlights and a lot of shouting over the intercom. He believes he may have been guilty of a little 'creep back' when he shouted 'bombs gone,' but he was not alone in this most heavily defended of targets. On the homeward journey Paddy allowed his thoughts to drift to those in the cities he had bombed. His memories of the blitz the Germans had inflicted on his home city, when he had seen the ruined factories, demolished houses, fires raging and a population which retreated nightly into the countryside, simply strengthened his resolve. Not all returned and Paddy again thanked heaven for his luck.

He had now completed twenty missions and although death was taken for granted, he was beginning to believe in his own immortality. Immortality did not linger in the thoughts of replacements to the squadron. They saw, as Paddy saw, that with a quick rub of a cloth a whole crew would be wiped off the board – either killed in action or missing. It was with a sweep of a hand that crews were obliterated at base. Yet what of those who may have survived? Talks had already been given on the problems aircrew would face should they be shot down over enemy territory and survive. Air-crew already carried escape kit and those that lectured believed that it was all so easy. Again and again those in power stressed that all that was required, if shot down, was to respond with name, rank and number. Such information would enable relatives to be informed of the whereabouts of such a prisoner. It all sounded so simple. The weather continued to dictate when they flew as Jack and his crew gathered strength for the next stage in the battle. On the 14th of January their target was Brunswick, situated in central Germany. It was a city of Messerschmitt factories and heavily defended. The pep talk at briefing had been given as the crew reflected on the task in hand. Freezing conditions on board did little to help. The cold air probed their inadequate clothing and slowed their reactions. The usual routine checks were made as the Lancaster, at full throttle, lurched into the sky. Not all were so lucky, as the load was heavy, and there were several crashes.

They had been ordered to fly a direct route to Berlin and then, before reaching the city were to turn south to Brunswick. Flak was hurled at the incoming bombers. The ferocity of the German attack caused bombs to be released some six miles from their target. The Lancasters had been harassed by enemy night fighters on the inward and outward trips, often with devastating results. Paddy could only imagine such an agonising death as he watched burning Lancasters fall out of control.

January 1943. 408 Canadian Squadran at Dalton Airfield.
Paddy is on the front row – seventh from left.

Although his aircraft had been hit by flak the crew survived and returned.

At 16.35 hours on the 20th of January, Paddy was again in action. The target – Berlin. This,they had been told, was to be a heavy raid with about eight hundred planes dispatched – Lancasters, Halifaxes and Mosquitoes. The latter were to be used for diversionary raids on Hanover and Kiel. Assembling over the North Sea, the bomber force, displaying no navigational lights, droned on its way, an anxious time for pilot and crew as a slight deviation by any plane could and did result in crashes. This was always a discouraging factor. Large numbers of bombers did not always result in greater destruction, Paddy remembers.

Although the weather on take-off had been fine Paddy and his companions flew into increasingly hostile conditions. Not only was the weather hostile but the German reception of the bomber force proved even more devastating. By continually attacking the bombers, before, during and after the raid, considerable damage was inflicted on them. Communication systems, especially the railways, had been bombed. Factories, including that of Roland Brandt, were destroyed. Brandts produced radar equipment and its destruction was a lucky strike by a wayward 4,000lb. bomb. Many bombs fell wide of their intended targets, over thirty aircraft were lost, including thirteen Lancasters, yet the mission was considered a success by those in charge. Paddy's plane, damaged by flak, returned to base to be patched up ready for another day.

This did not take long, for it seemed no sooner had he landed and nodded to the newcomers in the mess, (where he now felt a stranger) than he was again airborne. The proposed bombing raid was part of Bomber Harris's strategy of disrupting Germany's oil supply. Magdeburg, 60 miles south west of Berlin was an oil depot and railway centre. The briefing had gone through the sequences of navigation, weather, time of take-off, time over target and the usual talk of just how important the mission was. Paddy and his crew were tired, bloody tired. They knew how heavily oil installations were defended and that in spite of a proposed decoy raid on Berlin, Magdeburg would not be an easy target.

Linton-on-Ouse had really never slept since the increase in bombing raids. Those responsible for servicing the aircraft worked in shifts. Checks and yet more checks were carried out as the aircrews tried to get some sleep. Woken by a shake on the shoulder and a welcome cup of tea, Paddy heard again the dreaded words, 'It's time sir.' Struggling to come to terms with the glaring light, he drank his tea, washed, shaved and dressed. He remembered landing in the early hours of the morning and now he was preparing himself for yet another raid. The world seemed to have gone mad.

Magdeburg ... The crew had smiled grimly to themselves at briefing as they remembered their experience of other such towns. Paddy suddenly thought of Joan and cursed those who had posted her to Londonderry when he was in Yorkshire. Typical of the military mind he thought, as he listened to the chatter of his fellow crew members. That night there would be eight in the Lancaster rather than the usual seven. As Paddy looked round at his companions he wondered if this would alter their luck. Seven of the crew had that hunted look while their 'guest' showed an air of uncertainty. Three of the crew were members of the R.C.A.F., including Flight Lieutenant Dinning, (the guest) who was coming back to flying after an appropriate rest. Jack Mill the pilot, and Sergeant George Currie were the other two. Flight Sergeant Taffy Jones, rear gunner, Sergeant A.E. Elliott, Flying Officer G.M. Reid, Flight Sergeant Charlie Rankin, wireless operator, and Paddy were those members of the R.A.F. assigned to Six Bomber Command and the Royal Canadian Air Force

The all-important weather forecast was not encouraging. January was not a good month for flying. Fog generally lay over the Vale of York and German industrial centres were noted for their low cloud. Jack Mill was not happy with the flight test of the first two planes they were allocated. His word was law and Lancaster E.Q., B for Bertie, became their final assigned aircraft. The crew gritted their teeth for their take-off time was now 19.35 hours, some way behind the main force of attacking aircraft.

Magdeburg, as the crew had suspected, was a heavily fortified town. The diversionary raid over Berlin consisting of 22 Lancasters and 12 Mosquitoes proved of little use as the enemy night fighters hammered home their attack. Paddy saw plane after plane go down as he instructed Jack to 'keep her steady'. Hardly had he uttered the words, 'bombs gone,' than there was an almighty explosion as bullets winged their way into the Lancaster. Acrid fumes filled the aircraft while metal fragments spun in every direction. Over the intercom Paddy heard the screams of the rear gunner while at the same time noticing flames coming from the engines. Jack's voice could be heard shouting, 'I don't think I can hold it!'. Seconds later a further spray of bullets peppered the plane. One of these zoomed across Paddy's head and left him shocked and dazed. Without warning the plane went into a death spin. Slowly, with engines on fire the aircraft spun earthwards. Paddy tried desperately to make for the hatch but the doors were iced solid. Without warning a huge explosion ripped through B for Bertie and Paddy was catapulted into the night air. With the screams, curses and appeals to God of his fellow crew members ringing in his ears, he felt for his parachute – his last chance of survival. Hands frantically flaying, he felt for the release, found something and pulled. His body almost snapped in two as the parachute cracked open and he drifted away from the noise of battle towards the flames of Magdeburg.

Survival!

Chapter Eleven

Life seemed unreal as Paddy drifted in and out of consciousness. Through blurred eyes he recalls his frantic efforts to guide his parachute away from the burning town of Magdeburg and watching the debris of the bomber spiral to earth. Fear and terror gripped Paddy as he landed on German soil. He discovered he had landed in a village cemetery. While struggling from his parachute he spotted a fellow flyer a little distance away. Lurching towards the prone body he discovered a crew member – dead.

Gazing around, he looked at the sky above, chose a star, and tottered away from the burning town and the sound of children's voices. Keeping to the fields he watched, with some trepidation, hordes of people walking along the road. His fuddled brain failed at first to understand the reason for this and then he realised that he bore some responsibility for their plight, for had he not just bombed their town? Trying to remember what he had been told to do if shot down over enemy territory, he struggled on. Suddenly the sound of vehicles mingled with the noise of the refugees.

Startled, he was aware of a searchlight sweeping the fields. Paddy realised that he would, if discovered, get a hostile reception from those on the road. Certainly there was no guarantee that he would, if he put his hands up, be treated kindly. The searchlight came nearer and nearer and was about to come down on him when he spotted an abandoned plough and dived behind it. The beam of the searchlight swept over his prostrate body but no bullets followed. Heaving a sigh of relief at his luck, he lay still for a little while before he stumbled onwards.

In spite of his flying suit Paddy remembers the bitter cold. He had always believed, till now, that the Lancaster was the coldest place he had known. This cold seemed to get to the very marrow of his bones. Determined to stay out of the clutches of the searching Germans, Paddy sought shelter. Looming ahead he saw the outline of a building.

On closer inspection he discovered it was a barn and prising the door open, stepped inside. Stumbling about, he felt straw under his feet and sank to the floor. The relief at being out of the wind was overpowering and soon he drifted into a fitful sleep.

It was the cold that woke him. That and hunger. As the grey light of dawn crept into the barn Paddy took stock of his situation. He had his escape kit with its Ovaltine tablets, a map showing escape routes, water purifying tablets, a bottle of water and a compass. He wondered what help they would be as he touched his head where the bullet had almost killed him. He also examined his bruised and battered body for it was some hours since he had completed what was his first parachute jump. His thoughts turned to Joan and what message she would receive from those in authority. The straw he had slumbered in did not give the warmth of hay. Not only that but it seemed to irritate. Still, he was alive and that was something to be thankful for. Paddy decided to stay in the barn until dusk when he would make another foray and again follow his star.

Nodding off to sleep only to be startled into wakefulness as his body reacted to his predicament, he began to realise that he was not well. The day passed slowly as the cold continued to seep into his body. Taking what comfort he could from his Ovaltine tablets, he snuggled into the straw. Darkness came at last and with it a determination on his part to remain free. Creeping out of the barn he felt dizzy and after a few stumbling steps he fell. This happened not once but several times and must, he thought, have something to do with his head wound. His head throbbed and his chest was badly bruised from the straps of the parachute. Common sense told him he could not go on and he decided to give himself up. This was not as easy as he thought, for as he made his way towards the road a party of singing German soldiers passed him by and even though he must have presented an odd sight, they ignored him. 'So much for that" Paddy thought as he kept his star in sight.

Some time later a truck rumbled by then stopped. Uncertainty gripped Paddy as he stumbled forward uttering the words, 'English flyer.' The truck was a civilian one and the driver gestured to Paddy to climb into the back of the truck. Seeing that he was unable to do so, the driver took pity on him as he opened the cab door. No words were spoken but somehow Paddy knew that he would be handed over to the military. This proved to be the case and Paddy can only describe the days that followed as a battle of wills.

Sixty miles from Magdeburg Paddy was introduced to the ways of German interrogation. This was at Dulag Luft near Frankfurt-an-main. Taken roughly down some stone steps and locked in a cell, he waited. Hunger and cold gnawed at his bruised body but when asked for information he simply replied, 'Johnston, Pilot Officer, 656566.' Again and again he was taken from solitary confinement to be asked how he got into Germany, had he any contact with the underground and what was the strength of his unit. It proved an impasse as Paddy repeated his name, rank and number while quoting the Geneva Convention. Fed once a day with cold cabbage soup and a thin slice of black bread, he was determined to win the battle of wills. To do so he saved a morsel of bread so the guards would see him chewing as they thrust his daily meal into his cell.

Had Paddy known, he could have taken comfort from the fact that two German fighter aces had been killed in action on the night of January 21st. Major Heinrich Wittgenstein, with eighty-three kills to his credit, and Captain Manfred Meurer who had sixty-five enemy aircraft credited to his name.

The small high window in his cell allowed little natural light to penetrate. Lying on his thin straw mattress he had plenty of time to think. Determined to keep his mind active, Paddy wrote letters which would never be posted in the dust that littered the floor. He also made pictures with tiny pieces of straw from his mattress. Such activities stopped him thinking of those things he could not have. Sleep was denied him as the single bulb was switched on and off according to the whims of those in charge. What heating there was also fluctuated as the interrogators tried to prise information from him. Paddy also learned to give ample warning to his guards if he wanted to go to the toilets. Sometimes it seemed like hours before he was escorted out of his cell and to the toilets. Fortunately he did not suffer from diarrhoea and counted himself lucky. Conversation with those in adjoining cells proved difficult but the knowledge that others were in a similar situation added to his resistance.

Disorientated, he was asked to complete a form from the Red Cross which would enable his next-of-kin to know that he was alive. He refused as he suspected a trick and was shouted at with words he did not understand. The punishment and questions went on for days. Finally, after a period of intense interrogation, Paddy, still cold, hungry and dirty, was given a suitcase, clothes and a Red Cross parcel This seemed like a gift from heaven and at first Paddy was unable to believe his luck. He began to wonder if he had given the Germans information about his unit. He need not have feared for they knew from other sources that Paddy was a genuine flyer.

From the interrogation centre at Dulag Luft on the outskirts of Frankfurt. Paddy was given first class travel to his next destination, in a cattle truck. Before he boarded he asked his guard for permission to go to the toilet. This was granted and as Paddy went about his business a brush came between his legs and a German voice whispered, 'God save the King!' Paddy sat perplexed until he was called by his guard to, 'Come!' On the truck he mingled with other captured aircrew. Listening to the stories of others he realised how lucky he had been to survive. The cattle trucks were stationed in a siding near a chemical factory and no-one was more thankful than the young man from Ireland when the train moved off – destination unknown.

Back in Londonderry, Joan Johnston did not know what to believe. The message she had received from Linton-on-Ouse was that her husband had been killed in action. Comforted by her fellow Wrens and her family she knew nothing of the battle that had raged over the skies of Magdeburg. Like so many of her generation she held on to a belief that Paddy was, somehow, alive. The days grew into weeks with still no news. Then on the fourteenth of March she received a telegram which had been re-directed from Thirsk. With shaking hands she opened the envelope and read, 'From Air Ministry, 77, Oxford Street, W.1.,13/3/44. Information received through the International Red Cross Committee states that your husband P/O. William Johnston is a prisoner-of-war in German hands. Stop. Letter confirming this telegram follows. Stop.'

Great was the celebration among the Wrens at the Royal Naval Station, Maydown, Londonderry when her companions-in-war heard the news. Joan was granted compassionate leave and a posting was found for her nearer her home town of Thirsk.

Date	Hour	Aircraft Type and No.	Pilot	Duty	Remarks (Including results of bombing, gunnery, exercises, etc.)	Flying Tim Day	N
4-1-44	1950	EQT	P/O MILLS.	Bomb Aimer			
2-1-44	0040	EQT	P/O MILLS.	Bomb Aimer.	BERLIN OPS. 18	7	
2-1-44	2359	EQT	P/O MILLS.	"	BERLIN OPS 18	6	
6-1-44	0023	EQM	P/O MILLS.	"	BERLIN OPS 20 STETTIN.	8	
14-1-44		EQJ.	P/O MILLS.	"	BRUNSWICK OPS 27·18	5	
19-2-44	1125	EQT	P/O MILLS.	"	D.N.C.O.	·15	
20-1-43	1635	EQT	P/O MILLS.	"	BERLIN OPS. 19	7	
21-1-43	1935	EQ*B	P/O MILLS.	"	MAGDEBURG OPS 20		
					MISSING.		
					TOTAL TIME FOR JAN.	:15	34
					TOTAL OPERATIONAL TRIPS:- 20		
					HOURS:- 127·10		

O.C. "B" FLT. 408 SQD

C.O. 408 SQD.

Jan.22/44;Lanc.II, DS 790 `B'(10ops): Shot down Night trip-Magdeburg

```
Plt   F/L Mills, S.A.                              Cdn POW
Nav   F/O Reid, G.M.                               RAF KIA
B/A   P/O Johnston, W.                             RAF KIA
WAG   F/S Rankin, C.                               RAF MIA
A/G   P/O`Currie' Gordon      32, Saskatoon, Sask. Cdn MIA
A/G   F/S Jones, H.D.                              RAF KIA
GUEST.—FE F/L Dinning, J.B.    Calgary, Alta.      Cdn POW
```

EXTRACT FROM PADDY'S LOG BOOK TOGETHER
WITH EXTRACT FROM LINTON-ON-OUSE RECORD

Chapter Twelve

Herded like cattle and packed like sardines the human cargo of officers listened as the guards shouted to one another as they made a final check on their captives. After some delay the train eventually chugged its way out of the station. Rumours abounded but all agreed that they were travelling east. Just how far east was unknown but as the stench inside the cattle trucks began to take its toll Paddy, being small, felt at a distinct disadvantage. At times it did have its advantages but this was not one of those times.

To the prisoners it seemed a lifetime until the stuttering train, belching smoke, drew into a siding. Orders were shouted as the doors opened and those inside the cattle trucks almost fell out. Gulping in the sweet smell of fresh air, the prisoners were ordered to line up. Such orders were accompanied by the odd prod of a bayonet. Gazing round his new surroundings, Paddy saw a camp some way off. This was his first sight of a permanent German prisoner-of-war camp and it did not impress him. Carved out of a woodland clearing, Stalag Luft III presented a forlorn picture. Dominating the scene were the watch-towers. These tall, match-stick-like structures housed searchlights and armed men who could, if they wished, bring devastation to those inside the compound. Again orders were shouted as the newly arrived prisoners were lined up and marched through the gates. Once inside Paddy noticed the barbed wire, the huts and the mud.

Two tall, enormous barbed wire fences protected the camp. These fences were separated by bare earth and presented a formidable obstacle to any who might, according to the Germans, 'be foolish enough to try to escape'. Not only did the fencing present an obstacle to any escape but some ten yards inside the perimeter fence was a warning wire some two to three inches above the ground. The area between this wire and the main fence was forbidden territory. As a new arrival, Paddy was taken in hand and allocated a bed space.

Paddy decided to watch and wait. Watching, he discovered that the green-painted huts within the camp were built on stilts with only the stoves and ablutions area having a concrete base. Each hut was divided into small rooms inside which were a number of beds, a stove, used only in winter, and various items that the prisoners had made. Paddy admired their ingenuity as his eyes roved over bookcases, tables and cupboards. He learnt that there was plenty of bed space available as all American aircrew had been moved to a new compound. He also realised that he was the bearer of news from the outside world. His new companions did not wish to know the latest war news, indeed they appeared to have much greater knowledge about that subject than he did. What they wished to know was whether the theatres were open, what was playing and did they still serve good ale in the 'Alice'. Paddy was able to answer some of their many questions and they in their turn, answered some of his.

Stalag Luft III was situated on the outskirts of Sagan on the river Oder, in a heavily forested area situated on the eastern border of Germany some sixty miles from Frankfurt. Pine trees dominated the flat landscape and it was these trees that provided the timber to build the expanding prisoner-of-war camp. A number of compounds were built and these housed officers or enlisted men. The Senior British Officer, (S.B.O.) of Stalag Luft III was Group Captain H. Massey. He had developed a military relationship with the German Commandant, Colonel Von Lindeiner-Wildau. It was the role of the S.B.O. to negotiate with the Germans while trying to ensure that the Geneva Convention was upheld. He could also report matters of concern to the visiting powers and to the International Red Cross. Stalag Luft III was guarded and run by the Luftwaffe. Thousands of Allied prisoners were housed in the camp and many had been incarcerated there for a number of years. Stalag Luft III had been witness to many, many attempts to escape. One of the most famous of such attempts became known as 'The Wooden Horse', when three prisoners, Peter Howard, John Howard and Philip Rowe, helped by their many supporters, had dug a tunnel using a vaulting horse to camouflage the entrance and had escaped to freedom.

Paddy was allocated to Hut 106 in the North Compound. Hut 106 was situated in the north of the compound and was the furthest away from the Appel ground. This hut housed R.A.F. officers of many nationalities and their orderlies. He was surprised to learn that the camp was still expanding, and yet not surprised when he thought of the increasing number of air raids to which the Germans were being subjected. He also came across Jack Mill, his pilot, who seemed to be the only other survivor of the exploding Lancaster.

As in any camp there were a set of rules which were interpreted to suit the general welfare of those imprisoned. Paddy quickly picked up words like 'ferrets', (Germans who 'ferreted' about looking for methods which might be used for escape); 'stooge', prisoners who acted as look-outs. and 'kriegie' (prisoner-of-war). Other words such as 'goon' (a prisoners' term for a German soldier), and 'cooler' (a punishment block) soon became part of Paddy's vocabulary. Roll call was 'Appel', when all prisoners were expected to line up in the compound and be counted. This normally took place twice a day but could happen at any time, day or night.

Unknown to P/O Johnston he had arrived in Stalag Luft III at a time of great tension. For almost a year, hundreds of officers had been working on an escape project which would, if it went ahead, cause maximum disruption to the German war effort. The proposed method of escape was a series of tunnels designed to come up outside the wire. Three tunnels had been started named Tom, Dick and Harry. One had been discovered by the ferrets and one had been left as a decoy while work continued on Harry. An elaborate system of soil disposal had been devised while the lining of the tunnel meant that a great number of slats had been removed from the bunk beds and other sources. During the months of winter the tunnel had made good progress.

If what he heard was to be believed the 'Harry' tunnel was a feat of wondrous engineering. Its entrance from under a stove in Hut 104 was a masterful example of 'now you see it, now you don't'. About thirty feet below the stove, three chambers had been constructed. These enabled equipment to be stored, soil from the tunnel stored ready for dispersal, and an air pump constructed from kitbags and Klim tins, (dried milk tins saved from Red Cross parcels). Two additional passing places were constructed and known affectionately as Piccadilly and Leicester. As the tunnel progressed it was eventually around four hundred feet long with railway-type rails made from stolen wood. These rails carried small wagons, again made from illicit swag, filled with ex- cavated sand and tugged along to the main chamber. Here they were emptied and returned to the tunnel face. A series of electric lights lit this tunnel of defiance as it made its way under the wire and towards that elusive freedom.

Many, many prisoners were involved in supporting the proposed escape attempt. There were those who were skilled in forgery, nicknamed Dean and Dawson, preparing false documents, others applied their talents to producing civilian clothing, while yet others bribed guards for information.

Whatever was produced needed a safe hiding place. Some of the smaller items such as maps or compasses were hidden in hollowed-out pages of library books. False walls were constructed and larger items hidden in the cavity created. Many of the forged documents required up-to-date information. This was obtained from the guards who were bribed with food or cigarettes. An amazing number of items and information vital to the escape was acquired in this way.

Paddy, after listening to the many tales of those involved, admired those who day after day, week after week, month after month gave their time, energy and enthusiasm to the problems of excavating a tunnel as a means of escape. These men had learned the techniques of tunnelling and knew its pitfalls, perils and the importance of accuracy. The tunnelers were also aware of the likely punishment the Germans would inflict should they be discovered.

Behind such a scheme was the drive of Roger Bushell. This tall, broad-shouldered Squadron Leader, who had once flown Spitfires and had commanded 92 Squadron at Hornchurch, had been a prisoner-of-war since 1940. Paddy became acquainted with Roger as he strode round the circuit, always in earnest conversation with one of his team. The tunnels had been long in the planning. Hope and despair seemed to go hand-in-hand with the progress achieved and the setbacks overcome. Now in March 1944 they were nearly there.

Paddy had proved that he was not a German spy and those in charge believed that he was entitled to an explanation of some of the oddities of camp life. The fact that Roger Bushell was known as Big X did not surprise him for the man had a hatred of the Germans and a desire to cause them as much trouble as possible. Paddy was told that within each hut there was a Little X who helped to co-ordinate the work of the escape committee. He had by this time got himself involved with theatre productions but volunteered his services and for a time became a 'stooge'. His work for the theatre group involved the making of scenery. The skills he had learnt in Belfast now found a ready market.

March was a cruel month in this part of Silesia. Cold, icy winds brought low temperatures and snow. The snow made life difficult. In spite of its cleansing effect, the snow, when allied to the wind, sent icy particles hurtling on to exposed skin. Still, there seemed plenty to do if one had a mind to do it. Routine chores occupied part of the day. First there was the question of food – always a dominant topic in the camp. The International Red Cross, together with the International Powers, inspected the camp and made certain recommendations regarding various aspects of sanitation and prisoner well-being. These organisations also arranged the repatriation of those prisoners-of-war who, in the opinion of the authorities, justified such a move. The International Red Cross also supplied parcels to the prisoners. These contained commodities such as biscuits, cheese, chocolate, jam, syrup, condensed milk, sugar, tea, cocoa, dried eggs, oatmeal, rice, chopped ham and soap. Such parcels, packed in tea-chests, were made up by different countries and as a result varied in what they contained. The tea-chests provided ideal material for the skilled carpenters who worked in the theatre. The tins containing the food were made into a variety of utensils and escape equipment. It was assumed, wrongly as it turned out, that the Germans would issue a parcel a week to every prisoner. Often this turned out to be half a parcel or even a quarter. Frequently there were no parcels issued when some misdemeanour had been discovered. The parcels, together with the basic German ration of bread, soup and margarine, which was collected from the cook-house, kept the prisoners on the bread line. Whenever a parcel was handed out, a 'scrounger' would appear requesting items which the proposed escapees could take with them. These requests, though grumbled at, were never refused.

Each mess was responsible for the preparation of its own food. Great ingenuity was demonstrated as the meals were prepared and the food rationed to accommodate needs. Skill was needed when slicing the bread for it was impossible to ensure that each slice was exactly the same. Often cards were cut to see who would have first choice – the highest card having the privilege. Food, and the thought of it gnawed daily into the minds of the prisoners.

Other chores also needed attention. Personal hygiene was a priority. The threat of lice was always present and all were encouraged to shower. There were no shower blocks but Paddy and his fellow prisoners used the wash-house. This had three sinks and a system was devised whereby a tin pierced with holes could be tied to the cold tap – the only tap. This primitive method not only showered those partaking but the wash room as well. In winter the wash room was like an ice-box and after showering in such conditions and trying to dry oneself with a damp towel, it was clothes on and back to bed. In summer time the process was the same but the sun provided the warmth rather than bed. Washing and drying clothes with inadequate soap, hot water and equipment was part of daily life. Hot water was at a premium. When needed, buckets were placed in a queue the night before to ensure fair distribution of the heated water. Each owner of a bucket would hand it in at one window and take it, filled, from another. While queuing for this luxury the prisoners would occupy themselves either by chattering or reading the many notices pinned to the wall, – notices advertising items for sale or wanted, league tables or 'Dear John' letters. The latter always brought a response from those who read them, the usual one being 'He's well rid of her'. What passed for a washing machine was known as a 'dhobi stick'. This ingenious device was simply two different-sized tins nailed to the bottom of a pole. By pounding the dirty clothes with this, the lather produced by thin slices of soap did its best to clean. Most clothes which underwent this process remained a dirty grey. Still, they smelled sweeter.

Reading the official notice boards was a 'must' for many of the men. Lectures on a multitude of topics would be advertised, including languages, science and literature. One of the surprises Paddy encountered when he became more familiar with Stalag Luft III was the theatre. This was a fairly recent innovation and the theatre building had been provided by the Germans. It was actually two huts joined together. Those who were interested in the entertainment industry had previously been in other prisoner-of-war camps where they had put on simple shows.

The architects among the P.O.W.'s drew up the theatre plans while skilled men volunteered for the many jobs that had to be done. Those in charge of such work asked the Germans if they could slope the theatre floor. They agreed to this, little realising that such a slope had more advantages than just improving the view of the stage. Behind the stage were the workshops and dressing rooms. The tea-chests which had contained the Red Cross parcels were stripped down and made into rows of seats. The theatre group attracted a wide range of skills ranging from carpentry and, painting scenery to acting.

Paddy found there was a great interest in the performing arts. The camp theatre was able to accommodate an audience of up to three hundred and fifty. Wing Commander Lackin was in overall charge and costumes were either made or borrowed from civic theatres. Famous names who had yet to make their mark at home included Rupert Davies, Peter Butterworth and John Casson. Plays staged included 'Rookery Nook' by Ben Travers, 'Arsenic and Old Lace' by Joseph Kesselring and 'Pygmalion' by George Bernard Shaw. There were two full companies and generally two shows every four to six weeks. Each show ran for three or four nights and then the scenery was changed and new props built by Paddy and his colleagues. Theatre-going became an occasion when the prisoners would dress up, take their saved chocolate ration with them and relax. Not all they saw were plays. Music halls would also be billed where such talents as the Saxtettes, Ron Birch's band or Les Lucas and 'The Swing club' would perform. The instruments used were, in the main, supplied by the Y.M.C.A.

There were also the keep fit experts and the sportsmen. Probably the greatest way of passing the time was walking the perimeter. This was known as a circuit. On his first circuit Paddy was introduced to the do's and don'ts of life in a prison camp. Inside the perimeter fence and some three yards in, was strung a low wire. Should any prisoner step over this trip-wire without permission then he was liable to be shot. Appel, he was told could be called at any time, night or day, when he and the other prisoners-of-war were to line up in fives to be counted over and over again. Appels could last from half an hour to many hours depending on the circumstances. Paddy was also told that many of the guards had been bribed, and a number had nicknames such as 'Rubberneck', or 'Nosey'. He was advised not to talk to the guards as this might upset a system of obtaining information. On such walks one could see the world outside the multi-wired fence with its watch-towers and strutting guards. Sometimes a ferret would be seen crawling under huts or probing the ground looking for tunnels. German anger at some hurled insult would result in upturned beds and fruitless searches. In spite of what was offered, boredom, for many, remained the main problem.

Paddy chummed up with Willie Ross from Scotland. Like Paddy, Willie was newly married and his wife ran his grocery store while he was in the R.A.F. Willie had great plans for extending his store and before long Paddy and he could be heard discussing ideas on how to accomplish this.

Paddy wrote letters to Joan as often as he could. With luck he might get not only a letter, but a parcel from home. His letters were heavily censored while Joan, now stationed at West Hartlepool, received lots of advice. Many newspapers published advice. One article read, "In every P.O.W. camp in Germany there are censors whose duty it is to read all letters sent home by the prisoners themselves or coming in from relatives and friends. Some of these censors have an excellent command of the English language, some are not so good. All of them are very busy men tackling correspondence written in a language other than their own.

If you are writing to a P.O.W. do your best to help these censors, in your own interest, by writing as clearly as possible. Recently, the first letter sent by a father to his prisoner son was destroyed because the censors found it illegible, although some photographs which had been enclosed were handed to the lad.

If you can have your letters typed you should certainly do so. Keep them brief and do not send more than one or two per week. If you overload the censors, not only will your letters be delayed, but they will not be able to get down to the work of scrutinising outgoing letters.

Be careful too about enclosures. The only enclosures normally allowed are snapshots or unmounted photographs of a personal nature and also simple bank account statements. Perhaps you have relations serving with our forces in the Middle East and sometimes they send you airgraph letters. You must not forward these letters to a P.O.W. This is strictly forbidden.

And there is another simple point to be borne in mind. 'Stalag' is a German word meaning 'permanent camp'. It is not the name of a town, and it is insufficient as an address without the addition of the appropriate number. Every day the post office has to return senders letters that come to hand addressed merely to Stalag, Germany.

If the writer of a letter to a P.O.W. is serving in His Majesty's Forces, whether at home or overseas, he must on no account give the address of his unit. Instead he should state the address of a relative or friend in this country who is willing to send on any letters received from his friend behind the barbed wire of a camp in Germany. No attempt should be made to correspond with P.O.W.'s through people in a neutral country.

These regulations may seem a lot to remember but rules are necessary, and by following them you will expedite the transmission of mails to and from those of your friends and relatives who have been unlucky enough to fall into the hands of the enemy."

Sound advice perhaps but of the many letters written few were received. Joan was not only writing but knitting for her husband – jumpers, socks, gloves. Parcels were made up and sent. Some arrived amid great jubilation, others went astray.

In the North compound there was tension in the air. Rumours were whispered, added to, then rejected. The news from the hidden radios was of the continued advance in Italy and the bombing of Germany's heartland. Roger Bushell knew that the opportunity for some two hundred officers to escape from the North compound may never come again. Yet he had to consult, for conditions were not ideal. However, they never would be as he and Wing Commander Harry Day discussed the situation yet again. There was still much to do but the 24th March was undoubtedly the best opportunity. It was a night without moon and would give the forgers the chance to put a date on the papers and enable those who were proposing, once outside the wire, to travel by train, to use the timetables they knew to be accurate. The major problems were the snow and the fact that the Germans may discover Harry before the tunnel could be used. The Wing Commander gave his approval as the nerves in the compound were stretched to breaking point.

Paddy was aware, like others, of the escape although not part of it. Like others he was determined to do his best to help to make a success of the whole operation. Much had been achieved but much remained to be done as Hut 104 became the centre of attention. Two hundred men were dressed in garbs as diverse as a travelling salesman to that of an engineer as they filled the rooms and corridors. As well as the two hundred escapees in Hut 104 there were also many look-outs posted to give instant warning of any untoward German activity. Also in readiness were the prisoners known as 'Rent-a-Mob'. Members of this group could be relied upon to make as much noise as possible as diversionary tactics for those wishing to escape were implemented.

On Friday, March 24th the 'Great Escape' began, not on the hour that had been planned but thirtyodd minutes later. Just after 22.00 hours.

Flight Lieutenant Johnny Bull was first out quickly followed by Harry Marshall and then Flight Lieutenant Ernst Valenta. Body squirmed after body along the three hundred and forty feet of tunnel. The escape process was hindered by an air raid but as the night wore on, more escapees breathed-in the clear night air as they wriggled towards the woods and freedom.

The order was to seal the tunnel at 05.00 hours. Before this could happen a patrolling sentry spotted steam rising from a hole in the ground. This occurred at the same time as Flight Lieutenant Shand was crawling towards the woods. Suddenly all hell broke loose.

Life, Paddy remembers, was 'unpleasant' after March 24th. The German Commandant von Lindeiner was publicly removed from command and replaced by Colonel Braune. The Gestapo were, because of the large number of escapees, now involved. Appel after Appel was called as the prisoners-of-war were forced out of their huts to be lined up, counted and recounted The snow did not endear itself to those who stood there. Winter still gripped Stalag Luft III as the prisoners-of-war, inadequately clothed and fed, were screamed at, shouted at and surrounded by a circle of bayonets as they waited for the next incident.

It was not long in coming. On the April 6th, just before lunch, the Senior British Officer was summoned to the new Commandant's office. The news was grave. He was informed that forty-one of the escapees had been shot. Colonel Braune stated that none of the forty-one had been wounded and that he was passing on information from a higher authority. Braune also declared that no names of those who had been shot were available He who told the news, like the man he told it to, knew that it was murder and against all the principles of the Geneva Convention. When the news broke, Paddy recalls that all those in the North compound knew one of the forty-one or knew someone who knew one of them. They were not all British for among the dead were Australians, New Zealanders, Canadians, South Africans, Lithuanians, Czechoslovakians, Greeks, French, Polish and Norwegians – a truly international force.

Some days later the Germans pinned a list of those who had been shot onto the notice board. The list contained not forty-one names but forty-seven. A few days later a further list was pinned up, as Paddy recalls. This list added another three names to those already known. Those who had been on the run and then re-captured and returned to camp, thanked their lucky stars.

Paddy remembers the anger that spread through the camp, anger that had no outlet other than to hurl abuse at those who were supposed to protect them. It was a terrible time.

Chapter Thirteen

Spring followed winter as the fury of the camp internees abated. The prisoners-of-war remembered the evil act the Germans had committed and vowed that justice would eventually prevail.

For many weeks after the 24th of March, life in the camp became unreal. Prisoners were woken at any hour of the night and forced to stand in the compound while they were counted and recounted. Sleeping with clothes on became the norm. Not only were they counted but their belongings in the huts were turned upside down. Nothing was sacred. The boisterous behaviour during Appel had gone, for as Paddy remarked, 'You don't ask too many questions when you have a dog snapping at your heels and a bayonet prodding your flesh.' In place of the swagger that had been commonplace there was fear, hunger, distrust and hatred. The hatred had no outlet other than against those who repressed them. Every insult hurled by the prisoners at their captors met retribution.

Those in charge waited for that great healer, time. It was slow in coming but, helped by the spring weather, life slowly returned to some state of normality. Yet it was not normal. The 'Great Escape' became, for a time, the 'Great Depression'. The new Commandant, a Colonel Braune, proved much stricter than his predecessor. Group Captain Massey, because of a war injury, had been repatriated and his place was taken by Group Captain D.E.L. Wilson. Unknown to the Germans, a new tunnel named 'George' had been started. The entrance to this new venture was under a seat in the theatre. However there did not seem to be the same enthusiasm for the undertaking. This was partly due to the stricter discipline, partly to the threat that any escapee would be shot and partly because of the prisoners' knowledge regarding the continuing advance of the Allies.

Apart from the more frequent Appels and lack of parcels, life in the huts changed little. There were some good story-tellers in the compound and none better than Boyd Carpenter who slept in the bunk below Paddy. Boyd, known by his name 'Chips', was both wealthy and well-connected. Once the hut shutters were up, the door to the hut barred and the lights were out he would regale his companions with tales of dining in high places. He had the ability to recall each place where he had eaten and what had been on the menu. He could describe how the food had been prepared and what wine was drunk with each course. As Paddy said, 'These were mouth-watering occasions and very elaborate stories.' Chips also declared that he was leaving his wealth to Judy Garland, the film star.

The summer weather saw Paddy occupying his time in many different ways. He attended lectures on various topics. He remembers John Casson's lecture on 'Going to the Theatre', and another by a fellow prisoner 'On decorating a house'. He also took a great deal of pleasure from reading the German notice board where notices such as, 'It is illegal for prisoners to possess gunpowder or wire cutters,' appeared. One of the oddities of camp life was the 'Food Echo' and the 'Clothes Echo.' These were trading posts where everything was given a points value. The 'Echoes' were operated like the Stock Exchange and the market would fluctuate daily. Once 'Chips' Carpenter spent all the points that Paddy's room possessed on a real Italian officers uniform. Why he did so remained a mystery but the members of the room had a slim time until they amassed further points.

For a hectic fortnight Paddy was involved in an intense game of poker. Day after day the game went on with cigarettes and I.O.U.'s as the stakes. Food became of secondary importance as each call was made and fortunes won and lost. Eventually the whole thing collapsed as bets became evermore ridiculous. On another occasion Paddy was part of a crowd watching a cat play with a mouse. Where they had come from no-one knew but someone opened a book and bets were placed on the outcome. As usual the cat kept catching the mouse then letting it go until the mouse scuttled into some long grass. Mystified, the cat continued to search but the mouse had got clean away. A great cheer rang out from those who had bet on the mouse outdoing the cat.

The Red Cross, now aware of the aftermath of the 'Great Escape' provided the prisoners with a film show. This was held in the theatre and the film was 'Orchestra Wives' starring Glenn Miller and his Orchestra. Many of the prisoners had never seen him or even knew of his music. Nevertheless it was an opportunity to listen to some good music and see real girls on a screen. The Germans had arranged that a projector and screen be set up and two prisoners were put in charge.

The whole show started smoothly with a good picture but the sound, according to Paddy, was a great disappointment. The projector was on its last legs and the disjointed sound continued throughout the showing. At the end there was a huge round of applause and Paddy decided to stay for the second showing.

Physical fitness was not ignored. Daily walks round the circuit, sometimes in groups of six, helped fill the days. Paddy remembered the days of his youth, (he was now twenty five years old), and decided to enter a boxing competition. He does not know why he did this but perhaps it was to prove a point. The resultant bout against a fellow prisoner cost him two teeth, after which he decided to hang up his gloves for good.

One of the highlights of the lengthening days was being able to play gramophone records out-of-doors. Somehow Paddy and his room-mates had acquired a wind-up gramophone and some records. One of his favourites was 'Clair de Lune'. He remembers lying outside the hut gazing at the stars while listening to the record.

Life within the close confines of the huts resulted in a great deal of tolerance and intolerance: tolerance to eccentric human behaviour and intolerance to those one could not come to terms with for reasons one could not explain. The circuit was one of the saviours of such feelings, as was the limited freedom to be able to visit friends in other huts. At other times discussions would lead to arguments and occasionally fisticuffs. It was difficult to escape from confrontation as there was no hiding place. Often one member of a room would up sticks and depart for what he hoped would be greater understanding. Tolerance was not helped by the removal of so many bed slats for the tunnels. Just before the break-out Paddy had one board for his head, another for his hip and a slightly bigger board for his feet. As he says, 'It was not very comfortable and I sagged a bit in the middle but it was for a good cause.' As more and more raids over Germany continued, more and more aircrews, from planes which had been shot down, filled the camp. The news the crews brought with them reinforced that from the secret radios. Hopes of an early release from the camp began to circulate.

Old wounds were re-opened when the ashes of those who had been shot were returned to the camp. The news on the notice board tried to ensure that the men's spirits were not allowed to sink too low. Lectures continued as well as other group activities. The theatre crowd put on 'The Drunkard' produced by Billy Williams with Roy Wilkins as the Musical Director. This Victorian melodrama was played for laughs rather like a pantomime. The audience of 'kriegies' were encouraged to cheer the hero and hiss the villain. The moral of 'The Drunkard' was therefore lost on the prisoners but they enjoyed the performance.

The Classical Orchestra conducted by Arthur B. Creighton with its string, wind and brass sections continued to practice and give performances in the camp. Forty-one prisoners were members of the Classical Orchestra which gave its last performance on October 22nd, 1944. Complementing the Classical Orchestra was the 'The Happy Valley' Silver Band and many other musical groups.

Paddy recalls that some weeks before Christmas 1944 a notice appeared inviting anyone who was interested to join rehearsals for a performance of Handel's Messiah. Along with many others he joined the choir. The conductor was an officer from the London area whom Paddy remembers as Arthur. He proved to be a very experienced man in choral work and he soon sorted out the assembled recruits. Rehearsals were held in a warehouse next to the theatre. During a break Paddy caught sight of a vaulting horse. Further inspection revealed that it was the one used in the breakout from Stalag Luft III when the escapees had made a successful home run. Word quickly spread that the 'Wooden Horse' was still in existence and it became a talisman as prisoner after prisoner touched it for good luck.

Rehearsals continued and the day came when the soloists joined the choir. These were experienced singers and they were able to fill all the parts except that of the tenor. Every new arrival at the camp was questioned as to whether he was a tenor and had experience of performing in the Messiah. Fortunately a large party of American aircrew arrived, amongst whom was an experienced tenor.

It was decided that two performances would be given in the theatre. Because of the intense cold and lack of fuel, dress for the occasion was to be greatcoats, scarves, gloves and cap. The audience responded by dressing the same. Handel's Messiah was performed to a rapturous audience and Paddy was proud that he had played his part.

The improving weather brought out not only the dust but the sports-men. Paddy was told of the tremendous work put in by the prisoners to create a sports field. Like the camp, the sports area had been carved out of the forest. Tree stumps had been removed with shovels, picks and axes 'borrowed' from various sources. Once the holes left by the stumps had been filled and levelled, the field was used for soccer, rugby, American softball and in winter, skating and ice hockey. Leagues were established and placings of the various teams were pinned up on the notice board. The prisoners were delighted when the Y.M.C.A. solved one of their greatest problems – equipment. Those with talents in athletics could be seen practising the high and long jumps, throwing the discus or training for any event where there might be a competition.

Perhaps the best and certainly the biggest Sports Day was held in May 1944. Opened by a parade of competitors accompanied by the Happy Valley Silver Band it proved a talking point for days. Various athletic competitions were held. These ranged from races over 100 yards to 440 yards while the high jump or long jump occupied potential champions. To accompany such an athletic meeting, enterprising prisoners devised numerous side-shows. These included Treasure Hunt, Hula Hula Girls, Wheel of Fortune and many others. The currency for taking part was the cigarette. All profits were sent to the American Compound where cigarettes were in short supply. Some of the side-shows were dubbed 'the worst show in the world' and those who paid could do nothing but agree.

Cricket also played its part in healing wounds, for the Germans continued to be puzzled by such shouts as 'Out L.B.W.', or 'go to silly mid on.'

Queueing for showers, hot water or any other facility where demand exceeded supply did not change. The hidden radios continued to be the main source of information. Great was the jubilation on the 6th of June, 1944 when the Allied Forces, under the leadership of General Eisenhower, landed on the beaches at Normandy.

Paddy and his fellow prisoners now had a new hobby, that of mapping the Allied advance. In the Education block a complete wall was taken up with a large map which accurately reported the advances and retreats of the various armies. The Germans provided the ink and paper for the map denoting the area from Moscow to the North Sea. The lines of the Allies advance were shown by thread which was changed almost daily. The Germans took a great deal of interest and pride in the map even when the news portrayed was against them.

Proud of their loudspeaker system, the Germans played loud martial music which was relayed to the prisoners. As well as music, news bulletins in German were broadcast. The translators in the camp noted what was said and this was later read out to the prisoners in their huts. This was done to prevent friction.

The prisoners in Stalag Luft III were unsettled. News of Arnhem had been noted and no one was taking bets as to the length of the war. The day still began with the noise of the wooden bar on the outside door of the hut being removed, coupled with the shouts of the guards ordering the prisoners to get up. German winters were desperately cold and the majority slept fully clothed. Once the guards had cleared the huts the men would be lined up and counted.

According to those who held Paddy and thousands of others as prisoners of war, the shortage of Red Cross parcels was due in no small measure to the advance of the Allies. Instead of one parcel a week they were cut down to half, then a quarter size. Very few parcels arrived from home and letters too were in short supply. One policy that the prisoners shared with their captors was to waste nothing. One morning Paddy and his room-mates received an extra parcel with their German rations. The parcel contained dehydrated vegetables, unfortunately over-run with weevils. Never ones to miss an opportunity the cooks boiled the vegetables, killing off most of the weevils. Those that survived were spooned aside as the prisoners partook of the soup. Many of the plates and mugs used in the camp were made by cutting up the tins which came with the Red Cross parcels. The tins, once cut up, were flattened using stones. A little strip of grease-proof paper from the margarine wrapping was used to seal the joints.

Some of the older 'kriegies' were pastmasters with the tins. Perhaps the finest example of their ingenuity was the blast furnace type of stove. These small ingenious stoves were encased in a large jam tin with smaller, pierced tins arranged in a certain way and blasted with a hand-turned fan. This could ignite small twigs which created enough heat to boil a tin of water. There was little coal and as a result, work parties were organised to go outside the camp and into the woods to cut logs. This form of co-operation was of benefit to prisoners and Germans alike. Co-operation was not always the case. One of the biggest altercations with the Germans that Paddy remembers was when they insisted that all tins be returned to them empty. A food strike was called and eventually the order was withdrawn.

Stalag Luft III was some sixteen miles from the Oder river. For weeks all at Sagan had heard the sounds of the Russian guns. Their target, according to those who knew about such things, was Berlin. Warsaw had fallen and this victory had been marked on the map in the Education hut. Sagan was on the direct route to Berlin and this caused a degree of panic among the guards. Tales of Russian troops murdering, raping and robbing those who resisted their advance added to that panic.

The thunder of the Russian guns at Breslau, coupled with the rapidity of the Russian advance, resulted in the Germans deciding to evacuate Stalag Luft III. Little time was given to prepare for such an evacuation. The prisoners were ordered to carry as much food and clothing (a myth for little food or clothing was available). The Germans turned a blind eye as bunks, cupboards and eventually huts were demolished, for with snow on the ground the prisoners needed to construct sledges. The all-important currency – the cigarette – was also extracted from any Red Cross parcels and packed. Any cigarettes the prisoners had to leave behind were soaked in tanks of water to make them unavailable to the Germans. Knapsacks, sewn from tattered blankets, were also made. Time was of the essence as the Germans harried and hustled those they had been ordered to move.

Dawn came early as the ill-fed and ill-clothed prisoners were lined up in the cold, icy conditions and were warned about trying to escape.

Promises of an eventual train ride gave hope as the gates were opened and with the encouragement of a prod from a bayonet Paddy joined those on the road. There were few backward glances at the camp as feet shuffled along the icy road. The journey westwards proved slow and tortuous. The cold air probed their inadequate clothing. Driving sleet replaced the falling snow as a biting wind whistled through the trees. The wintry weather increased the misery of the hundreds of prisoners as they shuffled their way towards the unknown. A number of men became ill and were supported for many miles by others.

The pinched look on the faces of the villagers they passed made the prisoners realise that the local population was also in a serious condition. Under orders to dig trenches to stop the Russian invaders, the civilians went about their tasks in a most sullen manner but in any case, could do little as they too were surrounded by Germans with rifles.

The prisoners were told that they had to cover sixty miles, sixty miles of twisting, winding roads through unnamed villages. Snow and ice added to the discomfort of the prisoners, unused to walking long distances, as the Germans moved them on. No hot food was available and what bartering took place with the villagers produced little result. As the snow melted, the sledges, so hurriedly constructed, became a burden and were abandoned. Goods were transferred to any who could carry them. The agony of the march continued. Men were fainting not only from the cold but from pain and hunger. Paddy stumbled on with the rest, offering help as and when he could. Thoughts of food seemed to be uppermost in the minds of the marchers and many a meal was cooked and eaten in imagination. Blisters became the norm and those who had slipped on the ice had other injuries. Slowly the sound of the Russian guns diminished as each yard covered brought them nearer their destination – the railhead at Spemberg. They slept in barns, outhouses, fields and woods: the lack of food and proper accommodation began to take its toll. After five days of painful walking they reached their destination. Paddy never realised that a cattle truck could be so comfortable. Resting on a flimsy layer of straw he fell asleep.

On waking, Paddy was told that the train was now in a siding in Tarnstedt, outside Bremen. The cattle-truck doors were opened as the escorting Germans ordered the prisoners out. Again they were on the move. The road led upwards until a camp, the Milag, recently evacuated by prisoners from the Merchant Navy, was reached. Paddy remembers the nightly war against bed bugs which forced many to sleep under the stars. He also recalls having a grandstand view as American planes attacked the docks at Bremen in a daylight raid. Another fillip to their situation was the distribution of food parcels which enabled them to cook a meal and have a hot drink. The naval lads had also left them a list of contacts who would exchange cigarettes for food.

Paddy began to dream of freedom. It was not to be, for as the Allies advanced from the west, the prisoners were ordered to pack up what goods they had and be prepared to march. Unsure as to their situation, rumours spread through the camp that they were to be used as hostages. Their destination they were told, was Stade on the River Elbe, there to await a ferry. The news from the hidden radios was relayed through the columns of men. All knew, even their guards, that the war was almost over. They were ordered onwards and one did not argue with rifles.

Those in command tried all the delaying tactics they could think of. Being poked with a rifle caused resentment and hostility, especially when used against the sick and injured. In the end it was decided that it was easier to co-operate with those who shouted and screamed orders. The weather during late April and early May was warm and comfortable. The country fields and woods provided a stimulus that many of the prisoners had yearned for during their period of incarceration. The ebb and flow of light through the trees brought comfort to many.

As the march continued the Germans became more easy-going. The guards allowed a number under their charge to call at farms in order to barter for food. The farmers and their families, knowing that Germany had lost the war, were happy to oblige. In return for a note, often signed by Flight Lieutenant Joe Soap, food and drink would be obtained.

At night a bed was made from pine branches and ferns. As Paddy gazed at the stars his thoughts turned to Joan and home. Fortunately, he could not see how thin he had become although he knew he had lost a couple of teeth. He breathed in the smell of the pine wood and felt that his luck was holding. His body had adjusted to the daily walking and the irregular intake of food. Seven days had gone by before they finally arrived at their destination. Paddy recalls that the village houses on the outskirts of Hamburg had cart wheels on their roof. This enabled storks to build their nests and was believed to bring good luck to the house. It was something to hold on to.

The promised ferry boat did not arrive, so the next day they were marched to Blankensee on the outskirts of Hamburg. Told that R.A.F. prisoners would not be welcome in the city because of the bombing, a route skirting the city was devised. Missing a hostile reception and possible infection, the marchers made for Bad Oldstead. Here the sullen crowds indicated their hatred of the fliers. After a few hours they were in Lubeck which looked, from a distance, a delightful walled city but again they were warned that they would not be welcome. The leaders of the march made the excuse that the prisoners carried a fever.

Camp was eventually made at a deserted farm on a lakeside some ten miles south of Lubeck. The barns were full of milking cows whose bellowing to be relieved of their milk kept all but the deepest of sleepers awake. Among the groups camped by the side of the lake were some who were experienced in milking cows. Paddy certainly had no expertise. He only managed to obtain half a cupful of milk.

Within a few days, after a terrifying bombardment by Allied artillery, a tank pulled into the camp and the officer in charge told the men they were free. Unfortunately he also told them that they would not be transported home for another month. There was elation at the word 'free' but puzzlement at the delay. Accommodation was arranged at a comfortable army barracks in Lauenburg. There they listened to Churchill's speech when he declared, 'The German war is therefore at an end. After years of intense preparation, Germany hurled herself on Poland at the beginning of September 1939, and, in pursuance of our guarantee to Poland and in agreement with the French Republic, Great Britain, the British Empire and Commonwealth of Nations, declared war on this foul aggressor. After gallant France had been struck down, we from this island and from our united Empire, maintained the struggle single-handed for a whole year until we were joined by the military might of Soviet Russia, and later by the overwhelming power and resources of the United States of America. Finally the whole world was combined against the evil-doers, who are now prostrate before us'.

Churchill continued, 'We may allow ourselves a brief period of rejoicing, but let us not forget for a moment the toil and efforts that lie ahead. Japan, with all her treachery and greed, remains un-subdued. The injury she has inflicted on Great Britain, the United States and other countries, and her detestable cruelties, call for justice and retribution. We must devote all our strength and resource to the completion of our task, both at home and abroad. Advance, Britannia! Long live the cause of freedom! God save the King!'.

Things were about to change, for shortly after Churchill's speech an R.A.F. officer appeared stating that they would all be home for V.E. day. Paddy wondered if it was all true as wild excitement spread through the barracks. Thinking of the logistics of their situation he doubted whether it could or would happen. He was proved wrong for the next day all of the ex R.A.F. prisoners-of-war were taken by truck to an airfield sixty-odd miles away. Crammed into planes they were all familiar with, Paddy and his companions took to the sky. The aircraft were all manned by volunteers – a wonderful gesture. Landing at airfields in the south of England they received a heroes welcome. WAAFs formed up outside the mess door as if they were a guard of honour. As those who had been in Stalag Luft III walked between the lines, the lovely ladies squirted each and every one with flea powder!

A shower and a meal followed this unusual welcome home. Issued next day with clean clothing they were all given a medical examination.

Paddy, after three X-rays, was found to be reasonably fit. He was given leave, a railway pass to Thirsk and his beloved Joan. Although now in clean clothing, Paddy realised that he presented quite a different picture from the one Joan remembered. His gaunt face, prison haircut and missing teeth caused him some concern. He need not have worried, for Joan, who had been given an immediate discharge from the Wrens, was at the station to meet him.

The luck of the Irish had stayed with him.

Postscript

Following the unconditional surrender of Japan on 15th August, 1945 Paddy, along with thousands of others, was considering his next move. Prior to his demobilisation Paddy Johnston returned to Scarborough. This time it was not for a course for potential aircrew but to look at the options available.

Returning to the building trade did not appeal. Neither did staying in the Royal Air Force. Teaching attracted him and after completing various forms he was accepted as a student at Didsbury Training College. This newly formed Emergency Training College was set up by Manchester Education Authority and the Government to train teachers for the many vacancies left by the war.

Paddy was among the batch of 224 male students who were admitted on 31st of January, 1946 and guided through their studies under the watchful eye of the Principal, Alfred H. Body. Successfully completing the course, Paddy entered the teaching profession and eventually became Head of Remedial Studies at Thirsk School. Paddy Johnston retired from teaching in 1981.

As I write this Paddy and Joan have just celebrated their fifty-ninth wedding anniversary.

Geoff. R. Moore. October 2002. Thirsk

Bibliography

Air Crew – Bruce Lewis Cassell

The Bomber War – R. Neillands –
Murray

Lancaster at War – M. Garbett, B.
Goulding – PBS

The Longest Tunnel – A. Burgess –
Bloomsbury

The Hardest Victory – D. Richards –
Hodder & Stoughton

The Course of Irish History – Moody
& Martin – Mercier Press

This Sceptred Isle – C. Lee – B.B.C.

Pee-Tee. U.K. Cadets – Albany. Vol. 5

Wirebound World – Stalag Luft III –
H. P. Clark – Cooper & Sons

Second World War – M. Gilbert –
Weidenfeld & Nicolson

Up the Shankill – P. Hamilton –
Blackstaff Press

Shankill Road Mission Yearbook

Anti-Aircraft Artillery 1914-55 –
N. W. Routledge – Macmillan

Roof Over Britain – H.M.S.O.

Bomber Command – M. Hastings –
Michael Joseph

A Crowd is not Company – R. Kee –
Eyre & Spottiswoode

Wings Over Georgia – J. Currie –
Goodall Publications

The Berlin Raids – M. Middlebrook.
– Cassell

The Night Blitz – J. Ray – Cassell

Wings Over Linton – P. D. Mason –
Fenton Enterprises

Flying From Dishforth – W. Booth –
Silver Quill

*Aerodromes in North Yorkshire &
Wartime Memories* – D. Brown –
D. Brown

Wooden Horse – E. Williams –
Collins

Other Sources:

Log Book of William Johnston

Imperial War Museum

British Library

Central Library – Belfast

Thirsk Library

International Red Cross

Eden Camp

Elvington Air Museum

Interviews with:
William & Joan Johnston;
J.H. Burns; Margaret Josephs;
B. Reynolds; M. Sanderson;
Rose Stothard, R. Thorogood.